SILVER THREADS

A Personal Look at the First Twenty-five Years of the Registry of Interpreters for the Deaf

Lou Fant

RID Publications
Registry of Interpreters for the Deaf, Inc.
8719 Colesville Road
Suite 310
Silver Spring, Maryland, 20910, USA

Library of Congress Cataloging in Publication Data

Fant, Lou
Silver Threads: A Personal Look at the First Twenty-Five
Years of the Registry of Interpreters for the Deaf

Library of Congress Card No. 9060905
ISBN 0-916883-08-6

these words processed by PROLANCE
Sherman Oaks, California, (818) 783-3820

TABLE OF CONTENTS

FOREWORD

One of the purposes of a tapestry was to depict historical events for the illumination of the illiterate. It preserved with a picture of people, edifices, forests, rivers, animals, and the like, a story or an incident at a time when the written word was beyond the ability of most folk to read.

As I began this book, I hoped to create a tapestry in words of the birth and growth of RID, but I was soon overwhelmed. I lacked the artistry of the tapestry weavers, and, working alone, I quickly realized the undertaking would require far more time than allotted for its completion. Another obstacle to weaving a complete tapestry was the lack of documentation. Minutes of board meetings during the first decade and a half are not on file in the national office; minutes of the business meetings at most of the conventions are nowhere to be found, and may not have even been recorded. So, I took instead, a few threads and wove them across the history of RID, using them to tell the story of our growth.

The main threads of my narrative consist of how the organizational structure developed in search of its identity; RID's efforts to certify interpreters; and the code of ethics. I then took some shorter threads—deaf culture, specialization, local affiliates, and advocacy—to give more detail to the picture as it might look a few years from now.

Using only these few threads, I necessarily left out many events, forces, and personalities that have played their parts in RID's history. Other hands more able than mine will have to weave these into the overall picture. This incomplete tapestry, woven with my few threads, represents my perceptions, my interpretations, my opinions, and in no way reflect any official endorsement by RID. I hope it will stimulate thought and action.

HOW AND WHY WE STARTED

The weather was hot and muggy. I had been wearing the same clothes for two days, because the airline had sent my luggage to Chicago. People were beginning to keep a discreet distance from me. I would have avoided me too if I could have. That is my most vivid memory of the Workshop on Interpreting for the Deaf, held on the campus of Ball State Teachers College in Muncie, Indiana, June 14-17, 1964, during which the Registry of Interpreters for the Deaf (RID) was founded.

It is rare for one to recognize a historic event when one is in the middle of it. Only an uncommon mortal will have the presence of mind to document in detailed notes what is happening, what led up to the event, how the participants felt about it, and to speculate on the future course the event will take. Being a common mortal, with more pressing thoughts occupying my mind, I did what most of us did, just moved with the event without truly observing it. The founding of RID is but a hazy memory to me and I regret that I can give no graphic, dramatic, eye-witness account of what went on.

In my conversations and correspondence with some of the other participants, I am of the opinion that the occasion was not very dramatic nor exciting. It was not even a scheduled event on the agenda, and happened only because two participants, Edgar Lowell and Ralph Hoag, came up with the idea.

Lowell, then the Administrator of The John Tracy Clinic, knew no sign language and nothing about interpreting. He did, however, possess a keen mind and by questioning the participants, especially Hoag, the son of deaf parents and an accomplished interpreter, he acquired an understanding of the problems we were having in the field of interpretation. The major problem was the shortage of competent interpreters, so recruitment of interpreters and people to become interpreters were priority matters. Following hard on the heels of this would come the matter of training new recruits to become interpreters. Lowell and Hoag, then the administrator of the Grants-in-Aid Program for Training Teachers of the Deaf, U.S. Office of Education, agreed that some kind of organization seemed needed that could assess interpreter competency and maintain a registry of them so consumers could be assured of receiving quality service.

On the afternoon of the third day of the workshop, Lowell announced that there would be a meeting that evening at seven to discuss the possibility of forming an organization of interpreters. Lowell, in a personal correspondence with me, said jokingly that, "If it hadn't been raining, or if there had been something else to do, RID might not have started at that time." (Lowell) According to the minutes of the organizational meeting, "Very few of the participants of the workshop did not turn up both hearing and deaf."

Lowell presided over the meeting with Hoag as his interpreter. There is no record of his remarks, but we know that he did put before us an idea that he and Hoag had worked out for the establishment of an organization of interpreters. We all thought it was an excellent idea, so RID was born sometime between 7:00 and 9:30 the evening of June 16, 1964. Officers were elected and the first meeting of the board followed immediately.

"National Registry of Professional Interpreters and Translators for the Deaf

Minutes of Organizational Meeting

It had been announced during the Workshop on Interpreting for the Deaf held during June 14-17, 1964, in Muncie, Indiana, that all those who were interested in establishing a national registry would get together in the Conference Room at Ball State Teachers College at 7:00 P.M. Very few of the participants of the workshop did not turn up both hearing and deaf.

All of the following decisions were made into motions and carried but nowhere in the notes were any records of who made and seconded them.

Also during this meeting a declaration of membership was shown by raising our hands. All others, who were now considered spectators, were asked not to vote on any issues.

It was also agreed that there would be no haggling on the wording of anything and that the further decisions would be to agree upon the concepts and allow the Constitution and By-Laws Committee to do the wording as they see fit. The summary of this evening's meeting would simply be the guidelines for future rules and regulations.

Doctor Edgar L. Lowell, Administrator of the John Tracy Clinic in Los Angeles, California, took charge of the meeting. He asked that someone take notes of the proceedings since there was no assigned secretary to do so. The meeting was organized in a quick, efficient manner and several things were decided.

(1) The purpose of this organization is to promote recruiting and training of more interpreters for the deaf, both manual and oral.

(2) A code of ethics is to be developed by the organization.

(3) The name of the organization will be the National Registry of Professional Interpreters and Translators for the Deaf (further known as NRPITD).

(4) The fee of $4.00 is payable upon declaration as a member. Since this is a registry there is no real reason for much expense so there will be no annual dues at the present time.

(5) Several discussions were held on membership with the end result being:

(a) For the present, members here at the meeting will be given a chance to declare themselves as members of NRPITD and be known as charter members.

(b) There will be two groups of members. One group will be interpreters and the other will be sustaining members. The sustaining members will be those deaf who are present at the organizational meeting.

(c) Both groups will be given sponsorship privileges.

(d) Interpreters not present at this meeting but who wish to become members must be sponsored by one present member before midnight of December 31, 1964. These persons will also be considered charter members and have sponsorship privileges.

(e) Interpreters wanting to join after December, 1964, must be sponsored by two members of the organization.

(f) No other deaf person can be admitted as a sustaining member except upon resignation or death of the now present sustaining members. The group will be self-perpetuating.

(6) The officers shall be:
- (a) President
- (b) Vice President
- (c) Secretary-Treasurer
- (d) Two members-at-large, one of whom may be a sustaining member.

Doctor Lowell then asked for nominations for President. Kenneth Huff was nominated. Several others declined the nomination. Huff was elected by a unanimous ballot. Ken Huff then took over his duties as president and opened by first thanking Doctor Ed Lowell (who cannot be a member because he is neither an interpreter nor a deaf person) for his efforts in organizing this group into a national registry. President Huff then asked for nominations for Vice-President. Several nominations were made for this office and Doctor Elizabeth Benson carried the vote. Nominations were then made for Secretary-Treasurer. Mrs. Virginia Lewis was the only nominee so she also carried a unanimous vote. At this time, the secretary assumed her duties. After several nominations were made for member-at-large, two were elected. They were Mr. Frank Sullivan, Sustaining Member and Mrs. Lillian Beard.

The Executive Board is as follows:

President—Mr. Kenneth Huff, Superintendent, Wisconsin School for the Deaf, Delevan, Wisconsin

Vice President—Doctor Elizabeth Benson, Dean of Women, Gallaudet College, Kendall Green, N.E., Washington 2, D.C.

Secretary-Treasurer—Mrs. Virginia Lewis, Associates in Anesthesiology, 2516 Market Street, Youngstown, Ohio 44507

Mr. Frank Sullivan, Secretary-Treasurer, National Fraternal Society of the Deaf, 6701 West North Avenue, Oak Park, Illinois 60302

Mrs. Lillian Beard, 8217 Wier Drive, Houston, Texas 77017

It was suggested that we begin gathering material so as to have a workshop in the future to upgrade the interpreters and train those who would be interested in becoming interpreters.

The idea of an accreditation program was also brought up but if anything is to be done on this it will have to be in the future.

The possibility of asking the VRA to subsidize such a program was also considered but was also tabled.

President Huff asked for a short Executive Board meeting at the adjournment of this meeting. Also that the Board is ready to take the names and fees for all those who wish to declare themselves at this time.

There were 42 interpreters registered, 22 sustaining members and of the sustaining members 7 qualified themselves as interpreters also.

No receipts were given to the people at this time but the treasurer will mail them at a future date.

Respectfully submitted,

Mrs. Virginia Lewis
Secretary-Treasurer"

"Executive Board—Minutes   June 16, 1964

In the Executive Board meeting which met at 9:30 P.M. following the organizational meeting, President Huff appointed two committees. First is the Constitution and By Laws Committee consisting of Dr. Benson—Chairman, Mr. Louie Fant and Dr. Ralph Hoag. The second committee appointed was the Membership Committee with Mrs. Virginia Lewis—Chairman, Mrs. Lillian Beard and Mr. Frank Sullivan.

Needless to say, the work of these committees begins immediately and their work is apparent.

President Huff asked that the minutes of the previous meeting be sent to Jess Smith for publication in the Silent Worker and to Dr. Benson, Chairman of the Constitution and By Laws Committee.

A letter concerning our registry is to be written and sent to:

(1) all Associations of the Deaf
(2) all superintendents of Schools for the Deaf
(3) all known interpreters not present here.

Application blanks will be drawn up and sent out to all members to be filled in and returned. All future members will use the same application blanks. The applications should include among the name, address, etc. the following questions:

    (1) Can you interpret in court?
    (2) Can you interpret in large gatherings?
    (3) Can you specify the size groups you can interpret for?
    (4) Can you read the language of signs and finger spelling?
    (5) Can you interpret for religious gatherings?

President Huff also asked that we keep the dates of November 19 and 20 of this year open for a trip to Washington, D.C. The Executive Board has been asked to be consultants to "Captioned Films for the Deaf."

Respectfully submitted,

Mrs. Virginia Lewis
Secretary-Treasurer"

The founding of RID was an unexpected outcome of the workshop. It was, however, the next, logical step to be taken to carry out the purpose of the workshop:

"The purpose of the Workshop was to identify the occasions and situations in which deaf persons are likely to be at a disadvantage; to establish standards for interpreters for the deaf; to suggest training, curricula, and criteria for admission to training courses for interpreters; to develop a manual and/or other guidelines for interpreters for the deaf, both for the hearing and the deaf individuals involved; and to collect and identify the manuals and booklets dealing with dactylology." (Smith, p.v)

If RID had not been established at that time, it surely would have come about shortly afterwards.

I do not know how it feels to be a pioneer. It is doubtful that any of us gathered there on the Ball State campus saw ourselves as pioneers. We knew we were breaking new ground, but there is no way we could have imagined that we were setting in motion forces that would culminate in what RID is today.

Who were the people at Ball State? The proceedings of the workshop list 73 participants and 6 observers. As I looked over the list, I could readily identify 41 of them as people involved in the education of deaf children, as administrators or teachers. In other words about 56% of the participants were professional educators. In addition there were 15 deaf people who were not then in the field of education, but who had probably worked in a school for deaf children in some educative capacity at some point in their career. If I include them with those actively engaged in education, the total comes to 66 or 90%. I will deal later in the book with the impact of these educators on the character of RID in its early years.

Of the four official interpreters for the workshop, only one listed herself as an interpreter, the other three were one teacher and two school administrators. Two other participants called themselves interpreters. I mention these facts to illustrate that although most of the hearing educators in attendance could and did interpret, they did not think of themselves as interpreters. It is important to grasp this mind-set in order to understand the early history of RID.

We were eager to recuit, train and verify the competence of interpreters, but I do not believe we thought they would become full-time interpreters. It is my opinion that we perceived the new interpreters functioning in much the same way as we had, that is, holding full-time jobs and interpreting on the side. We probably thought that new interpreters would be recruited mainly from the field of education. Critical to the development of a body of full-time interpreters would be the amount of work available and compensation.

The volume of work was increasing, but had not yet reached a size that would support more than a handful of full-time interpreters, and these would be employed mainly in institutions of higher education. We did anticipate that the amount of work would increase considerably, but I doubt any of us foresaw the explosion of employment opportunities that took place in the seventies. What we envisioned was an upgrading of interpreters and recruiting of new interpreters, mostly from the ranks of good signers who showed potential. There was some attention given to recruiting people who knew no sign language, but even these, I suspect, were expected to support themselves at other full or part-time jobs.

The papers delivered at the workshop covered such areas as materials available for teaching sign language, particularly filmed material (video tape was not yet a feasible option), qualifications and competencies of interpreters, recruitment and training, interpreting problems, and communicating with deaf people at all levels of language competencies. There were three papers, two from England and one from Russia, which were in the printed proceedings of the workshop, but were not delivered during the workshop because their authors were not in attendance. The two from England described the interpretation scene there, and the one from Russia, a long one, about the use of "the hand alphabet" with "speech gestures," did deal with interpretation in Russia, but the bulk of it was about the thought processes of deaf people and how these manifest themselves in their sign language.

As I re-read the proceedings of the workshop, there seemed to be as much emphasis on sign language and communication with deaf people as there was on interpreting. The speakers' expositions of sign language, its varieties, how it is used, and so on reflected that we had gone about as far as we could in describing sign language in non-technical terms. Our thinking was stalled and needed a breakthrough, a new perspective, in order for the public to understand more completely and accurately what sign language was and how it operated. None of us were trained in the science of linguistics, and sign language was not recognized as a language by the field of linguistics.

In 1960, William C. Stokoe, Jr., then head of the Department of English at Gallaudet College, published a monograph (Stokoe, 1960) which was the first attempt at a linguistic analysis of ASL. I doubt that most of the workshop participants had read Stokoe's work, and even if we had, we were skeptical of his conclusions. But, the time was right, and we were ready for the infusion of a whole new way of thinking about ASL. Within a few years, we were to abandon our inadequate concepts about ASL, our cumbersome ways of describing it, and wholeheartedly endorse the linguistic approach to the study and explanation of ASL. Our concern, one might say, preoccupation, with sign language is illustrative of how an idea, whose time had come, had reached full-term and was about to be born.

ORGANIZATION

Prelude

The interpreting scene prior to 1964 was so vastly different from that which exists today that it is a strain on the imagination to contemplate it. No one worked full-time as an interpreter and to say that anyone worked part-time is misleading. When one says that one works, it is understood that some type agreement exists between the worker and the employer as to what work is to be done and how much remuneration the worker is to receive. Such was not the case in those days. We did not work as interpreters, but rather volunteered our services as our schedules permitted. If we received any compensation it was freely given and happily accepted, but not expected.

The question of compensation was dealt with by declaring that interpreters ought to be paid for their services most of the time. Adequate compensation was focused primarily on legal matters, and little attention was given to other types of interpreting situations. Everyone agreed that compensation was a good and necessary thing, but scant attention was given to whether it would be enough to induce people to be full-time interpreters, nor was there much discussion about who would pay for the services. Compensation was something that everyone hoped would be resolved, but no one knew, nor was anyone eager to speculate on how it would be resolved.

Interpreters today might wonder why interpreters of yore were not paid. First, remember that there were few people who called themselves interpreters; there were many who could interpret, but few of us saw ourselves as interpreters. We earned our living as school people, rehabilitation counselors, religious workers, or were primarily housewives. We perceived our work as interpreters as just another way of helping deaf family members, friends, co-workers, or complete strangers. It was a way of contributing to the general welfare of deaf people, not a way to make money, much less earn a living. We did not expect to be paid, we did not ask to be paid, because we did not do it for the money. We felt it was our obligation, our duty to do it, and if we did not do it, the deaf person would suffer and we would feel responsible.

We had grown up in an era when charitable activities were primarily private endeavors, not public undertakings. There were no United Ways, Community Chests, and other such organizations which took responsibility for looking after the welfare of the underprivileged. Good deeds were a matter of private, not corporate concerns. There were such groups as the Salvation Army and the Red Cross, but their resources were limited to attending the destitute in times of dire crises. We were conditioned to believe that, because of our education and privileges, we owed something to the community. Wealthy people made donations to worthy causes, and if one was not wealthy, one donated one's skills. Interpretation was one of the ways we repaid our debt to the community.

We were considered by the hearing and deaf communities to be competent simply because we worked with deaf people. In cities where there was a school for deaf children, agencies would call the school for help anytime they were confronted with a deaf person with whom they could not communicate. A teacher or dormitory counselor would be dispatched at no loss of pay, to interpret. No one asked us about our qualifications. None of us was a trained interpreter, so there was no feeling of need to be recompensed. I believe it was because of these feelings we all carried with us that we did not come up with more concrete proposals for compensation. The nearest we got to it was to suggest that a committee be chosen to study the problem, and that a pay schedule might be set up that would recommend interpreters be paid $10 an hour, or $50 per day, plus expenses, which were the going rates in some areas of the country. These rates were considered to be generous at that time.

While I was teaching at the New York School for the Deaf (Fanwood), for example, a group of students from Gallaudet made a field trip to New York city and were in need of an interpreter. The leader of the group contacted Dr. Daniel Cloud, superintendent of Fanwood, and asked if he could spare one of his teachers to interpret for them. Dr. Cloud asked me if I were interested, and it seemed to me a pleasant break from teaching, so I agreed.

The students were business majors at Gallaudet so their itinerary included visits to a number of financial institutions. Among the most interesting was the vault of the Federal Reserve Bank where I saw bricks of gold bullion--something I never would have seen otherwise--and a stop at the New York Stock Exchange. Our group stood on the visitors' balcony of the Exchange, and my interpreting aroused the curiosity of a large number of the people on the floor. Alan Crammatte, one of the teachers with the group, remarked that for a few seconds we probably sent a minor shock wave through the transactions of the mighty Exchange.

The field trip lasted two days, and each day I journeyed from my home in Yonkers, twenty or so miles north of Manhattan, by train. At the conclusion of the field trip, the group gave me a fine, expensive pipe which I enjoyed for years. There was no reimbursement for the train fare, and I doubt Fanwood was compensated for the expense of hiring a substitute teacher during my absence. Still, I did not feel exploited nor, I am sure, did Dr. Cloud feel ill-used. That was standard operating procedure at the time. Schools donated their time and skill as a matter of course.

On another occasion, while I was teaching at Gallaudet, several deaf faculty members asked me to interpret a class they wanted to take at the University of Maryland. I consented and went with them for one semester to interpret. I received their genuine appreciation for my interpreting, but no fee. I was not upset, because fees were not expected; that was simply how it was done.

I interpreted weddings, funerals, faculty meetings, workshops, conferences and court cases, rarely receiving more than a gift in token of the deaf person's appreciation. My work as an interpreter reflected the situation of all interpreters. We were volunteers who expected nothing in the way of financial compensation for our work. There were several reasons for that state of affairs: One was tradition. Since that was the way it had always been done, no one thought much about changing it. Interpreting was simply what one did as one's overall commitment to one's work with deaf people.

Another reason we were reluctant to ask for pay was the knowledge that the money would come from the pockets of the deaf consumer. We knew that the earning power of deaf people was such that to pay us would place a financial burden upon them. Our consciences prevented us from asking for fair and just compensation for our labors, so we accepted, without asking for it, whatever they gave us--gifts, money, or just heartfelt thanks.

A third reason undergirded both of the above. It stemmed from our backgrounds and our perceptions of deaf people. Most of us were children of deaf parents, and had grown up interpreting for them and their friends. To refuse to interpret would have been a serious breach of etiquette and considered a lack of gratitude. Furthermore, most of us had a strong religious upbringing which imbued us with a powerful sense of altruism and duty. Interpreting was one of the ways we kept the commandment to honor our fathers and mothers. We carried this on into adulthood and would have felt pangs of guilt from an indignant conscience if we had demanded pay for interpreting. To have asked for pay would have made us feel that we had somehow betrayed our parents. It is difficult to appreciate the strength of this impulse if one has never experienced it, but this, more than any other thing, explains the attitude we had towards charging a fee for interpreting.

Another force that shaped our attitude was our perception of deaf people. We grew up in an atmosphere suffused with patronization. Nearly everyone in our society looked upon deafness as a debilitating condition that had to be corrected. Deaf people were the unfortunates and had to be taken care of. This frame of mind was reinforced by professional educators of deaf children, and the teachings of our religious institutions. So as adults we saw ourselves as helpers, available any time, day or night, to assist deaf people out of their difficulties. We were not just interpreters, but aides.

I am of the opinion that we who were gathered at Ball State did not perceive ourselves as launching a new profession. We included the word in the name of our organization, The National Registry of Professional Interpreters and Translators for the Deaf, but I believe we were thinking of a professional interpreter strictly as one who was skilled, competent, and qualified. Some of us may have dared to envision the day when there would be full-time practitioners, but those were private dreams, and they never received official sanction by the organization.

Two factors lead me to believe that we did not see ourselves as setting up a profession. The first is the fact that within six months we changed our name to the Registry of Interpreters for the Deaf, dropping the word Professional from the title. The new name better expressed our intention to recruit, train, and maintain a registry.

The second factor is that eight years elapsed before we began to certify interpreters. There can be no profession without some type of examination to determine one's fitness to practice as a professional. There had obviously been a change in our perception during those eight years, and certification was clearly the next move towards professionalization.

With all of this in mind—the tradition of volunteer service, our upbringing, the prevailing view of deaf people, our concept of the organization's purpose—it may be easier to understand why we faltered as we took our . . .

First Steps

We had only vague notions as to what the organizational structure of RID should be, or of the mechanics of how it should operate. For the next three years (1964-1967) we were an organization of members scattered across the country with little, if any contact with each other, held loosely together by the occasional publication of a newsletter.

About the only concrete manifestation of RID was its board, which was autonomous. All decisions were to be made by the board and any input from members was only advisory. There were two reasons why we decided upon this arrangement.

One was alluded to above: We were too few and dispersed over too much territory to be able to confer with each other. It would have taken much too long to reach a decision about anything. It was, in short, just not practical to believe that we could arrive at decisions within reasonable lengths of time, whereas the board could.

The other reason was that we were, by and large, of like mind about what decisions needed to be made. We knew that whatever the board decided would be pretty much what all of us collectively would have decided anyway, so we felt no threat in letting the board decide for us.

During this period, three workshops were held that gave shape and form to RID. The first was a Follow-Up Workshop on Interpreting for the Deaf, held at the Catholic University of America, Washington, D.C. January 26-29, 1965. The first order of business was to change our name. The first name, The National Registry of Professional Interpreters and Translators for the Deaf, grew out of the perception that interpreting and translating were two distinct acts.

"Differentiation exists between an *interpreter* and a *translator* described as follows:

1. A *translator* renders the original presentation verbatim.

2. An *interpreter* may depart from the original presentation to paraphrase, define, or explain. He also presents or interprets, on the intellectual level of the individual or

audience, without regard to the language level of the original presentation.

The method of interpreting or translating may be manual and/or oral. By manual is meant the use of fingerspelling and the language of signs." (Smith, p.1)

The misuse of the word, "translator," is characteristic of a problem RID has had to this day with defining terms to describe our work. We attempted to rectify this error with the term, "transliterator," about which more will be said later.

This workshop produced our constitution (Appendix A) and first bylaws. (Appendix B) One of the major items to take note of in the constitution is found in Article V, Section 2, which says that, "Authority shall be vested in the executive board to govern this organization, by directing its policies and operations in all matters relating to the purposes for which it was formed." The same principal is echoed in the Bylaws, Article IV. We recognized that the organizational structure was too indistinct at that time to be able to take concerted action; therefore we opted for oligarchic, rather than democratic, authority.

Another document to come out of this workshop was a list of "some of the things that appear to some of us, who have had experience in interpreting, as important items to be considered" for the development of a code of ethics. (Taylor, p.29). "Miss Lottie Riekehof was appointed as a committee-of-one to develop such a code." (Taylor, p.32)

This workshop also made plans for the two other workshops which further defined our organizational character. The second of these is usually referred to as The Maine Workshop. The purpose was, "to develop a manual and a curriculum for training interpreters." (Taylor, p.40)

The participants met for more than three weeks, July 7-27, 1965, at the Governor Baxter State School for the Deaf, Portland, Maine, and produced the manual, *Interpreting For Deaf People*. (Quigley) This manual served as "The Bible" for a number of years and exerted much influence upon our thinking. The results of Riekehof's work appears in the manual as our first code of ethics. (Appendix D)

The document produced at the Maine Workshop was designed as a guide to what an interpreter training program ought to include. Under the heading "General Aspects of Interpreting," are the following topics:

Physical Factors in Interpreting
Platform Interpreting
Fingerspelling as an Interpretive Medium

Interpreting for the Orally Oriented Deaf Person
Interpreting Idiomatic Expressions
Interpreting for Deaf Persons with Severely Restricted Language Skills

This section is followed by one on "Specific Areas of Interpreting," which covered legal, medical, religious, job placement, counseling, and psychotherapeutic settings. Then came a section called "Program for Training Interpreters," which was a suggested curriculum. Keep in mind there were no training programs in existence at that time,* but the development of this model curriculum clearly indicates that we expected to institute them shortly.

We had only vague ideas about where these programs would be situated; the guide mentions adult education programs, colleges, universities, churches, and schools for the deaf as possible sites. Financial support for the programs, it was hoped, would come in the form of grants from vocational rehabilitation agencies. It would be quite a few years, however, before sufficient funds from the Federal Government would be available to set up training centers. In the meantime, sporadic training probably took place, using this manual as the official guide, but I was unable to find documentation of their existence in the files of the national office.

Except for a few items, the contents of the manual are still pretty much the backbone of today's ITPs. The most noticeable difference is that today we treat ASL as a language with a focus on the study of its structure. The manual has long been out of print, but if a copy can be obtained by interpreter trainers, it is worth a study; it still has some valid things to say about the skills and knowledge interpreters ought to have.

---

*From personal conversation with Dr. Lottie Riekehof, it would appear that the first interpreter training program for college credit was at the Central Bible Institute in Missouri, which was begun in 1948. This predates the formation of RID by sixteen years.

16

The third workshop, A Workshop to Activate Interpreting Services for the Deaf, convened in San Francisco, July 9-11, 1966 at the Sheraton Palace Hotel. The major outcome of this workshop was a resolution which led eventually to the establishment of a home office for RID.

"Whereas the Registry of Interpreters for the Deaf has been in existence since 1964, and
Whereas the R.I.D. officers are composed of dedicated individuals with other full-time responsibilities, and
Whereas this has led to only the most minimal services being provided to date, and
Whereas vitally needed interpreting services continue to go unmet due to a lack of staff and effective machinery to identify, plan and carry out interpreting services to the deaf, and
Whereas the NAD and R.I.D. have demonstrated a capacity for working in harmony;
Therefore, be it resolved that the R.I.D. and the NAD jointly assume responsibility for improving interpreting services for the deaf by a cooperative effort to obtain VRA grant to support:
a. A full-time staff to operate out of the NAD home office.
b. This staff would plan and carry out workshops and training programs as determined by the NAD-RID and funded by the VRA.
c. It would carry out research and demonstrations and related activities as determined by the RID-NAD.
d. Serve public relation functions and other steps to improve interpreting services for the deaf." *(A Workshop to Activate Interpreting Services for the Deaf, p.29)*

Over the next year, NAD prepared a grant proposal and submitted it to the Vocational Rehabilitation Administration of the Department of Health, Education, and Welfare, to set up and staff a home office for RID. The grant was awarded and took effect July 1, 1967. It was an annual grant, renewed for five years.

The grant made possible the hiring of our first Executive Director, Albert T. Pimentel. The home office was located in NAD's offices. It is fitting that we pause here to express gratitude for NAD's valuable assistance in getting RID on its feet. Appreciation is also expressed to the Vocational Rehabilitation Administration (VRA), not only for the grant to establish our home office, but also for funding the workshops that led to the founding of RID and the nurturing of its growth.

(handwritten marginal note: When was NAD established?)

The beginnings of RID occurred during the legacy of the Kennedy and Johnson administrations, when large grants were available to assist handicapped people. Kennedy began this outpouring of funds partly because he had a mentally retarded sister. The sweeping legislation for civil rights under the Johnson administration included rights for handicapped people. RID was a beneficiary of the efforts of these two presidents. There was not a time before, nor has there been since, when so much money was available to insure that handicapped people would have so many opportunities. It was truly a golden era as far as federal funding was concerned.

One effect of this great outpouring of federal money was that it produced more deaf students desirous of additional education and training. Numerous community colleges began accepting deaf students into their programs. One large institution, San Fernando Valley State College (now California State University, Northridge) in Los Angeles began to accept deaf students, and another large institution, the National Technical Institute for the Deaf, was founded as a result of the quest for more educational opportunities for deaf students. Naturally these programs created more jobs for full-time interpreters.

During his tenure, Pimentel concentrated on organizing state chapters of RID. The Texas Society of Interpreters for the Deaf was organized in 1963, a year before RID, and became the first local affiliate of RID. The first local affiliate organized under the aegis of RID was the Southern California Registry of Interpreters for the Deaf, which took place in 1967. Since the founding of SCRID, the number of affiliated chapters has grown until today they exist in forty-seven states and seven provinces of Canada.

During the seventies, RID faced its most trying time, financially. The grant from VRA expired in 1972, and there were no funds available to maintain a fully staffed home office. We operated with part-time secretarial help and with dedicated volunteers who would come to Washington from all over the country to work for a week or two. We began an odyssey of moving from NAD's headquarters to whatever space was available at Gallaudet University. If it had not been for Gallaudet's generosity in providing office space, and some financial assistance from NAD, we surely would have reverted back to our status in 1964, or even expired altogether.

The eighties saw the dawning of a new era for RID. Financial woes continued to plague us, but there was the faint beginning of a turn toward a new attitude among the membership. RID was about to undergo a transformation in its character which would alter its course significantly.

From the establishment of our home office in 1967 until 1970, little was accomplished in bringing the membership into closer contact with each other, except for the establishing of local chapters. In 1968, the board decided that RID would have biennial conventions beginning in 1970, in Delavan, Wisconsin, and thus provided the machinery that has done more to chart the course of RID than any other single event.

The purpose of the earlier conventions was to share information about who was doing what around the country. There was not much focus on the interpretation process until the Rochester convention in 1978. At this convention there was increased attention on ASL itself. The 1980 convention in Cincinnati saw a heavy concentration on ASL and linguistics.

In addition to the increased focus on ASL, linguistics, and the interpretation process, there appeared also papers and workshops about the birth and development of systems for manually coding English. At the first convention, one paper was delivered on Seeing Essential English, and another on Cued Speech. I understand from personal informants that the 1976 convention in St. Petersberg, Florida, had several papers and workshops on the MCE's that had sprung up. Unfortunately the proceedings of that convention were not published.

The issue of whether ASL was a language, seems to have come to a head at the 1978 convention in Rochester. Recognition of ASL as a language can be implied from the titles of two papers: "Some Structural Characteristics of American Sign Language," by Joan Forman and Frank Caccamise, and "American Sign Language (ASL) Technique in Interpreting/Translating," by Sharon Neumann Solow. The fact that Neumann Solow added the "(ASL)" might indicate how this new name had not yet achieved instant recognition in the field. George W. Johnston delivered a paper entitled, "American Sign Language is English," in which he took an opposing stance to the idea that ASL was a language on its own merits.

It was during the late seventies and early eighties that argument over the legitimacy of ASL reached its peak and then faded away leaving ASL a recognized language by an overwhelming majority of the people in our field. In the field of education, however, there is a sizable number of people who still do not accept ASL as a language.

Among the ten conventions RID has had, none stands out as prominently as the 1980 convention in Cincinnati. The meeting and its aftermath resulted in a profound change in RID's structure. As the members gathered in Cincinnati, most of them had but one issue on their mind: the oral interpreter question.

It is interesting to note that at this convention there were quite a few papers dealing with linguistics, and with professionalization. Four special interest groups met, and there were nine meetings, each entitled "Special Issues Forum," one of which dealt with oral interpreting certification. From this apparent small place in the whole convention proceedings, one would never suspect that this was "The Big Issue."

In May of 1979 the board had approved and adopted a proposal from the Alexander Graham Bell Association for RID to certify oral interpreters. Opponents of the proposal were determined to bring the issue to the floor of the general business meeting and reject the board's decision. Proponents of the proposal were equally determined to sustain the board's action. The battle lines were drawn.

On the last afternoon of the convention the issue was raised and to say that it was a heated debate is to put it mildly. Emotions reached astronomical heights, and personal recriminations were slung about with abandon. There was no professional parliamentarian on the scene, so Robert's Rules of Order bit the dust, all but dead. The board was even accused of having altered the minutes of their meeting at which the proposal was adopted. The accusation declared that in reality the proposal had been rejected. Even to this time, many members find it hard to forgive other members for things said and done that afternoon.

The convention was set to adjourn at four-thirty, and as that hour arrived, a motion was made and passed to adjourn. This brought on a tremendous chorus of objections from the anti-proposal contingent. Some stood in their seats and yelled, others sat and openly wept. The scene resembled a swarm of angry hornets whose nest had been disturbed. In spite of the tumult, the meeting stood adjourned and the proposal stood as adopted by the board.

The incandescent anger of the foes of the proposal resulted as much from their frustrated efforts to bring the issue to a vote as from their objection to the principle of certifying oral interpreters. Had they been able to achieve a victory, however, the bylaws at that time gave autonomous power to the board. The board was not obligated to accept the vote, so it was possible that, defeated on the convention floor, the board could still put the proposal into action. This knowledge aggravated the bitterness the opponents felt toward the board, and a genuine threat to secede from RID to form a rival organization was narrowly averted.

The shock waves of that turbulent afternoon shook the organization to its roots. The uncertainty felt as to whether RID could survive was palpable. The fact that RID did recover was due largely to the fact that a resolution passed at the 1983 convention in Denver to revise the bylaws was accepted by the board. It is to the board's credit that it accepted and approved the new bylaws, which stripped it of its autonomy. Had the board denied the resolution, or rejected the new bylaws, RID might well have withered away. So, in the long haul, the conflagration in Cincinnati brought about, or at least hastened, a needed revision in the structure of RID.

It is probably safe to say this controversy could not have happened prior to 1978, because ASL was not then fully legitimized. The debate could not have taken place until there was a sufficient number of members who, (1) accepted ASL as a language, (2) saw the act of interpretation as a movement from one language (ASL) to another (English), and (3) believed that interpreters, by definition, dealt only with languages. By 1980, there was a sufficient number to create a critical mass that exploded.

It is my opinion that the explosion in Cincinnati had as much to do with the increased desire to professionalize interpretation and to gain control of the organization as it did with opposition to oral certification in itself. From this perspective, the rebellion was a success, because at the very next convention, Hartford 1982, the board approved a reorganization of RID which divided the country into five regions, with an elected representative from each region to serve on the board.

Although representation was significantly increased, the power base was not. All control still rested in the hands of the board. That changed a year later.

The Next Step

In the beginning, there was cause to feel that RID was something that existed apart from us, the members. There was an identifiable entity, the board, which was all powerful, and made all the decisions for us, even ones that were extremely unpopular with large segments of the membership. There was some justification for the development of an adversarial attitude between the board and the membership, between "them" and "us." We spoke of the board as if it were RID, and of ourselves as belonging to it, but not of it.

There can now be no cause nor justification for that kind of mentality. We are RID. No one else pulls the strings; no one else decides the course we shall take; no longer ought we to say that, "RID must do such and such," with the thought that anyone other than ourselves must do it. The board is no longer our opponent, adversary, or master, but rather our representative body, elected by us to carry out our wishes.

Unfortunately, a large portion of our membership still carries deeply embedded memories of our early history. Old injuries and injustices are not easily put aside. The wounds have healed, but the scars remain. It is more difficult for some of us to release the past and work for a future that may not be what we once envisioned. New challenges face us now and still newer ones await us beyond the horizon. We shall be ill-equipped to cope with them if we carry with us the excess baggage of past inequities and unfairnesses, real or imagined.

We have now a well defined organizational structure with bylaws, officers, committees—standing and *ad hoc*, affiliated chapters, and special interest groups. Those are the bones and we are the muscles and organs that make the structure work. There is a feeling, however, that something is missing. We might compare the missing element to the mind, that intangible component that guides the organism, that gives purpose to its work, that has self-awareness. We may compare the "mind" to a philosophy that provides a rationale for our organizational structure, and it is that vital component which is missing.

"During the 1983 Biennial Convention in Denver, the membership participated in a goal-setting activity that yielded three primary goals for the RID: a standard, valid and reliable national evaluation system; a sound organizational structure, including a revised set of By-Laws; and a statement of the organization's philosophy. Four months latter, an *ad hoc* committee was appointed to develop a Philosophy Statement for RID." ("Straw Vote on RID Philosophy Statement")

Two goals have now been completed: the establishment of a new evaluation system and new bylaws. One remains, the statement of our philosophy. One might legitimately wonder why, after eight years, have we not achieved this goal? Possibly we have failed to appreciate its prime importance. It is logical that a clear statement of philosophy should have superseded all other goals, for they should draw their rationale from the philosophy. Our goals did not, however, grow out of our philosophy, providing yet another example of how we have historically dealt with issues and crises, by resorting to the most expedient solutions.

"In April 1987 the proposed statement was sent to all Affiliate Chapter Presidents, chairpersons of Special Interest Groups, and 25 randomly selected Associate members (5 from each region).

These 83 individuals constituted the national review body for the proposed Philosophy Statement. The responses to this review were as follows: 7 from Affiliate Chapter Presidents, 3 from Associate members, and 2 from chairpersons of Special Interest Groups." ("Straw Vote on RID Philosophy Statement")

The fact that only 12 out of 83 individuals asked to review the proposed statement responded, illustrates the low priority assigned to the endeavor. We do not esteem its value because we do not realize its import.

"Although the end product will be no more than one paragraph in length, its implications will be far-reaching. RID's formal Philosophy Statement will be a strong determining factor in our organizational structure, our activities, our budget, and our image." ("Straw Vote on RID Philosophy Statement")

If a philosophy is to have the profound impact on RID, as is suggested by the above quote, how can we give it anything less than our full attention? All other issues should yield to this one. We should put on hold any further major decisions and activities until this one has been accomplished.

Why We Need a Philosophy

There has been much discussion in recent years about our identity and our roles as interpreters. There seems to be a great deal of confusion as to who we are and what we are supposed to do. Our expectations and the expectations of our consumers do not jibe. Without a philosophy to guide us, such confusion is to be expected.

Every mentally competent individual's behavior is determined by her/his philosophy of life. Few individuals, however, are aware of their philosophy; it exists only in the subterranean world of their unconscious. They go through life with only a cloudy understanding of why they behave as they do. The same is true for organizations and institutions.

If an organization has no stated philosophy, then its method of operating stems not from a rationally, logically arrived at set of beliefs and values, but rather from an amorphous conglomeration of dimly perceived beliefs held by individual members. It is inevitable that the organization shall experience much discomfort, many false starts, and numerous occasions when it seems to be going off in all directions at once. If the organization, like the individual person, is to move along its own path, rather than be sidetracked by expediency, it must have a clearly articulated philosophy.

The first step toward defining and identifying ourselves as professional interpreters is to know what we believe in. Achieving awareness of ourselves is tantamount to knowing what we value. A philosophy sets forth our priorities for all to see and know what to expect from us.

Towards a Philosophy for RID

A philosophical statement is not a setting forth of purposes, objectives, or goals; these are derived from the philosophy. Neither can there be a statement of philosophy before it is clear what that philosophy is. We have put the cart before the horse by asking the Philosophy Statement Committee to draw up a statement of our philosophy by studying our bylaws. The bylaws are the cart, the philosophy is the horse, so it is understandable if the committee found its task somewhat puzzling. The statement they proposed is cited below:

> "A-]- The Registry of Interpreters for the Deaf, Inc. is an organization committed to furthering the profession of interpretation of American Sign Language and English and transliteration of English. In order to accomplish this goal, the organization shall strive to:
>
> B-]- promote the highest standards of integrity and performance of interpreters and transliterators;
>
> C-]- encourage continued professional growth and development of its members;
>
> D-]- foster a respect and understanding of cross-cultural communication, and
>
> E-]- advance an understanding of the profession and issues related to the process of interpretation and transliteration."
> ("Proposed Philosophy Statement of RID, Inc.")

The first thing wrong with the proposed statement is that it reflects an attempt to condense a philosophy into a single paragraph. The committee may be forgiven for this since that was their mandate. It is not possible, feasible, practical, nor desirable to condense our philosophy into one short paragraph. It would be of no value to us, even if it could be done. We cannot have a document of only a paragraph's length that "will be a strong determining factor in our organizational structure, our activities, our budget and our image." If it is not a full blown document stating our beliefs about crucial items, it will not help us to know ourselves.

The second thing wrong with it is that it is nothing more than a re-stating of our goals, along with suggestions as to how we intend to achieve them. We have confused "goals" with "philosophy."

A philosophy provides justification for what we do; it explains why we behave as we do; it is the rationale for our actions. A philosophy of a particular field of study, such as a philosophy of science, or economics, does not attempt to explain the phenomena* of God, man, and the universe, but rather the principles that underlie the field and guide its activity. RID's philosophy must address itself to what we believe about the phenomena of our field. We must answer such questions as: What do we believe the act of interpretation to be? What does it mean to be a professional interpreter? How do we perceive deaf people? What do we believe ASL to be? What do we believe about advocacy? The answers to these and other questions will more clearly define who we are, why we do what we do, what our roles are, and what consumers can expect from us.

Our Perception of Deaf People

To illustrate the type of analysis that I believe is needed to formulate the philosophy of RID, I shall explore three of the questions listed above: How do we perceive deaf people? What is ASL? and What is interpretation? I do not pretend that the illustrations are exhaustive, only that they are examples of what we must go through in order to have a meaningful philosophy.

---

*In classical philosophy, phenomenon means "any fact, circumstance, or experience that is apparent to the senses and that can be scientifically decribed or appraised." (Websters New World Dictionary, Second College Edition.)

Historically, hearing people have viewed deafness as a physical disability, a handicap, an aberration which precludes normal human development. Deafness was seen as a biological abnormality to be treated by a medical-clinical approach. If deafness was not amenable to treatment, and hearing was beyond restoration, then the object of treatment was to ameliorate the handicap as much as possible in order to reduce its effect on the deaf person's development. The thrust was to minimize the disability and restore deaf people to hearing society, that is, to make them as much like hearing people as possible. Harlan Lane gives us an eloquent description of this attitude and the ramifications it has had on deaf people in his book, *When the Mind Hears*. (Lane)

Lane begins with the premise that his book "is a study in the anatomy of prejudice." (Lane, p.xiii) He argues that people have a deep and abiding fear of diversity and are capable of extreme measures in their efforts to eradicate it. The fear of diversity moves people to oppress those among them who are different from the majority, and their buzz words are "assimilation" and "integration." To make them as we are is the ultimate goal, anything less being intolerable.

For deaf people this prejudice is most noticeable in the long history of the attempts of hearing people to suppress ASL. Nothing calls attention to their difference more dramatically than does their language. To acknowledge the legitimacy of ASL is to rob the majority of the driving force of its prejudice. But full-scale frontal assaults against it proved futile, so instead, hearing people took an oblique attack.

The need for sign language, the dominant hearing society argued, springs from the inability of deaf people to hear, and thus acquire the spoken language of hearing people. If the ears do not hear, supply them with hearing aids; teach the eyes to complement with lipreading the diminished power of the ear; train the tongue to utter the sounds of hearing people; in short, make deaf people as much like hearing people as possible. At least as much like them so that the differences between the two become minimal. The problem is the ear that does not function, so focus all efforts towards remedying that unfortunate condition, and thus remove the need for sign language.

"Where Clerc saw difference, Bell saw deviance; the one had a social model of atypical people, the other a medical model. For Clerc, deafness was, above all, a social disability; the great problem of the deaf was the hearing world in which they were a minority; he hoped for a day when hearing people of goodwill would remove the handicap by accepting deaf culture and language. For Bell, deafness was a physical handicap; if it

could not be cured, it could be alleviated by covering its
stigmata; hearing people of goodwill would aid the deaf in a deni-
al of their particular language and culture, in 'passing' as hearing people in a hearing world." (Lane, p.340)

Instead of seeing deafness as largely a problem of overcoming language barriers, we were deflected into seeing it as a problem of physical
disability. As a result, instead of deaf people being treated as a linguistic minority, of which we have many in this country, they have been
categorized with and treated as physically handicapped people. "As long
as this establishment (otologists, audiologists, speech pathologists, and
special educators) clings to the medical model, it cannot take the next
step forward with the signing community, which is to supplant that
model." (Lane, p.xiv)

RID's philosophy ought to spell out in unambiguous terms its perception of deaf people as seen through a model other than the medical- clini-
cal-physically handicapped model. Only then will we lay a firm foundation for the professional attitude we seek which will eradicate the last
lingering vestiges of the helper syndrome.

In a brilliant collection of articles by James Woodward, *How You
Gonna Get to Heaven if You Can't Talk to Jesus, on Depathologizing
Deafness*, the effects of the perception of deafness as a physical patho-
logical condition is lucidly explored. The most telling consequence,
however, is what that approach does to us, the hearing people.

"In addition to being detrimental to Deaf people, the handicapped classification of Deaf people is also detrimental to Hearing people. This detriment to Hearing people is more subtle, yet
perhaps more serious. By labelling Deaf people as handicapped,
we reject Deaf Culture, Deaf values, and the self-worth of Deaf
people. By saying Deaf are handicapped we are saying they really
are inferior. By using the term handicapped, we have placed
ourselves, consciously or unconsciously, in the role of
oppressor. We have said Deaf people have a 'deficiency, especially an anatomical, physiological, or mental deficiency, that pre-
vents or restricts normal achievement.' We have thus made it
clear that Deaf people can succeed only if they follow Hearing
rules and only to the extent they can become like Hearing
people. When we send Deaf children to doctors before we try to
find Deaf and Hearing adults for them to communicate with, we
have made deafness into a pathology, a sickness, that our science
feels it must eradicate." (Woodward, 1988, p.76)

If we perceive deafness through the physical disability model, it is well nigh impossible for us to avoid the patronizing attitude toward deaf people which they abhor and we claim to abominate. Yet, the physical disability model seems to predominate in both the deaf and hearing communities. To whom, for example, do we turn for funding of programs for deaf people? Overwhelmingly it is to those agencies set up to provide assistance to the physically disabled, the vocational rehabilitation programs. From whom do we get most of the financial support for deaf educational programs? Again it is the agencies designed to provide help for children with mental and physical disabilities, the special education programs.

In this decade of the eighties we are witnessing the birth of a different perception of deafness, one that does not focus on ears that do not function, but rather on minds that can be developed. It is loosely called the deaf culture movement, and it is rooted in the concept that deafness must be viewed as a sociolinguistic phenomenon. It views deaf people as being more closely allied with the cultural minorities in our society, than with the blind, the orthopedically disabled and the numerous others with physical disabilities. It asks not for recognition of the need for physical accessibility or restoration to society, but rather for the recognition of its uniqueness in human society, and the opportunity to demonstrate its ability to nurture the development of its members into productive, well adjusted members of society.

RID's philosophical statement must include what we believe to be true about the nature of deafness. If we support the physical disability view, then we as interpreters are little more than crutches, wheelchairs, and prostheses for physically disabled people. We become instruments to assist the physically disabled and must be willing to provide services in addition to interpretation.

If we support the sociolinguistic view, we function as cross-cultural mediators, providing communication accessibility to members of different cultural entities. This role does not proscribe the rendering of services in addition to interpretation, but rather limits those services to accessing information for members of the hearing and deaf cultures.

Our Perception of ASL and Interpreting

The sign language we taught in pre-Stokoe days was what is presently labeled, Pidgin Sign English (PSE). We called it by various names such as formal sign language, proper sign language, and educated-deaf sign language. The sign language which we now call ASL was referred to as, "real deaf sign language." The term "real" did not imply "genuine," but rather "truly," in the sense that it was the language of those who were really deaf and who had only a tenuous hold on English. Our nomenclature unwittingly contained subtle value judgments which clearly indicated which of the two we thought was the better.

A casual review of the sign language books published before ASL gained recognition as a legitimate language will reveal that instruction consisted primarily of mastering sign vocabulary. Lists of nouns, verbs, adjectives, and prepositions along with fingerspelling exercises were the main fare. Once these elements were learned, we might teach an advanced class in which sign idioms and slang were introduced.

When students brought to class examples of signing that departed considerably from English syntax, which they had picked up from deaf people, we explained them away by saying they were the products of deaf people who simply did not have fluency in English. We did not do this in disparagement of deaf people, but rather felt it was not their fault they could not follow English word order. Without realizing it, we were encouraging a sympathetic, patronizing attitude toward deaf people, and reinforcing an underlying perception of them as poor unfortunates.

Classes in sign language were generally taught by hearing native signers. No one had any training to teach, we just launched out with whatever material we could find, or made up our own syllabi as we went along. Most of the classes were held in churches, or church-related institutions, a few schools for deaf children, and private homes. Rarely, if ever, did one receive compensation for teaching a class.

While I was teaching at Fanwood during the mid-fifties, a week-long workshop was held for vocational rehabilitation counselors. The purpose of the workshop was to provide the counselors with an orientation to deafness, and in the process it was deemed advisable to teach them a little sign language. Dr. Cloud asked me if I would like to teach them one hour everyday; I thought it might be interesting, so I agreed to undertake my first attempt at it. I have no recollections of what I did, but I am certain I taught lists of sign vocabulary which I made up myself. For my efforts I was paid the monumental sum of one hundred dollars. I call it a huge sum because it was almost equal to half my monthly salary. Other than the fact that I was handsomely paid for my paltry efforts, this incident pretty well illustrates the state of sign language instruction at the time.

As I said earlier, prior to 1964 the books that existed for teaching sign language focused on teaching sign vocabulary; they were in actuality nothing more than dictionaries, not text books. The first of these was, *The Sign Language: A Manual of Signs*, by J.S. Long, published in 1918; in 1923 the Reverend J.W. Michaels published his book, *A Handbook of the Sign Language*; the Reverend Dan D. Higgins published *How to Talk to the Deaf* in 1942. The late fifties saw a trickle of new publications, then by the mid-sixties a flood of books hit the market. They were all dictionaries, though some of them made modest attempts to provide drills and exercises to practice. Some of them even contained lessons, but the emphasis was on memorizing vocabulary and stringing them together in English word order.

The one exception to the dictionaries was *The Language of Silence*, by Roger M. Falberg, published in 1963. This was the first book published that attempted to teach ASL as a language. Falberg's book was the first one to explain such ASL features as time indicators for tense, how to deal with space, directionality of verb signs, negation, and interrogative statements. He might have been the first to say in print that, "Signs do not stand for words. Signs, like words, stand for things and events." (Falberg, p.8) This simple statement indicates a profound departure from the way we had been viewing sign language. In these few words, sign language was severed from English. If signs stood for referents ("things and events"), and not for words, then they stood alone, independently, as the building blocks of a language in its own right. At the time, this was heady stuff and shook many of us out of our slumbering ideas about sign language.

Falberg, who was deafened during adolescence, says that sign language ". . . stands for a way of life that is dynamic, vital and meaningful; it points to a pathway wherein lies delivery from stultifying stagnation." (Falberg, p.ii) The dawning of awareness was beginning to illuminate our minds as to the crucial role ASL plays in the lives of deaf people. Falberg does not mention Stokoe in his book, so it is probable he had not read Stokoe's work, yet it is clear they shared perspectives: One, that of the scientist; the other, that of the practitioner. They were integral parts of that fermentation in the early sixties that eventually culminated in the elevation of ASL to its proper place in the family of languages, and in the formulation of the bases for the study of deaf culture.

The quotation cited earlier on page 13 reveals how we perceived ASL in 1964. Patently, we did not conceive of it as a language. Although Stokoe had already published his groundbreaking work four years earlier, we were unconvinced by his evidence. When we spoke of ASL as "sign language," we simply meant it was a means of communication through the use of signs and fingerspelling. To us, "sign language" was used metaphorically in the same way we speak of music or paintings as languages. Information and emotions are effectively expressed through them, but they are not languages in any linguistic sense.

Stokoe had sounded the alarm, but we did not take it seriously, and so proceeded down a path that led to a veritable morass of misdefinitions, such as those quoted on page 13, and misinformation that has hounded us to the present day. As we moved into the seventies and began to realize the enormous error we had made, we retracted our original definitions and conjured up others that, if not blatantly wrong, were just as obscure as the earlier mistakes.

Steven Fritsch-Rudser (Fritsch-Rudser) appealed to RID to stop using terms which we define for ourselves, but which run contrary to standard usage. This is wise advice and had we exercised more care in expressing our beliefs we might have avoided, or at least lessened, the confusion we are experiencing with regard to our self-identity. We interpreters, whose stock in trade consists of words, ought to be more circumspect in our use of them. Expediency has caused us to coin new terms and redefine old ones to meet new circumstances, which, rather than throw light on what we do, results in darkening the scene even more.

It is doubtful that any member of RID today harbors any reservations regarding the legitimacy of ASL as a language. Nevertheless, we persist in speaking of it as if it behaves in ways that other languages do not. In particular we go to great lengths in explaining that ASL stretches from some point called "pure" ASL to an opposite extreme called Pidgin Sign English (PSE). This misperception forced us to label ourselves as "interpreters of ASL" or "transliterators of PSE," and in so doing we further clouded an already muddy picture.

There is no such thing as "pure" ASL any more than there is such a thing as "pure" English. There is good ASL, fair ASL, and poor ASL, grammatically speaking, but there is no "pure" ASL. When someone talks about "pure" or "real" ASL, they generally mean that which is used by deaf people in relaxed, social settings, or the sort of ASL used for telling stories and jokes. A moment's reflection should reveal that to depict ASL as grammatically correct and good only when it is used in those circumstances demeans the language.

It is a fact that as ASL was being recognized as a language in the late sixties, there were many deaf people who refused to use it in formal, public circumstances, such as lectures and dramatic stage productions. This may have been the result of years of conditioning by hearing people that ASL was inferior to English. Deaf people have often expressed a sense of guilt when they used even English-like signing, and to use ASL made the feeling even worse. There are still thousands of such deaf people around today, and we must respect their feelings. Though we hearing people may not be blamed for perpetrating the travesty, we are nevertheless, recognized by deaf people as belonging to that majority which subjected them to the brain-washing, so they might be forgiven if they are still somewhat tenuous about our acceptance of their using ASL.

On the other hand, there are those deaf people for whom English-like ASL is the preference. Most of them are quite adept at ASL, but simply find it more comfortable to express themselves in an English-like version of it. It is difficult to see how they can be criticized for this choice. Do we not elect to speak in various styles of English depending upon the occasion and our mood? I always select the style of ASL used by the deaf person to whom I am talking or interpreting for as the appropriate style to use. We should accommodate ourselves to their choices without comment or making a value judgment.

There seems to be an obsession that drives us to protect ASL from any incursion of English that will contaminate ASL. Is ASL such a fragile thing that we must erect barricades to safeguard its identity? Perhaps we suffer from the "new convert" syndrome and strive to be more orthodox than the long-time practitioner. In terms of human history, our recognition of ASL as a language took place only moments ago. Perhaps we are still too excited about it and in our exuberance have gone too far in an effort to divest ASL of any influence from English. We must now exercise calmer, more reasonable judgment about what ASL actually is.

The use of the adjective "pure" implies "proper," or "correct" ASL, and that any other variety is "improper," or "corrupted." Whether intended or not, we are making a value judgment when we use "pure" to describe ASL. Let us rather use some such term as "standard" ASL and remove any judgment as to its quality or value. Let us not suggest, or even hint, that those deaf people who prefer a more English-like variety of ASL are using a debased language.

I believe it is even demeaning to refer to English-like ASL as PSE. The term "pidgin," has an intrinsic suggestion of arrogance and superiority to my ear. I hear it as one more manifestation of the dominant hearing society applying pressure on deaf people in an attempt to convince them that ASL is, after all, just sub-standard English. There is a remnant of condescension in the use of "PSE" which implies that those deaf people who use PSE do so because they are not fluent in English.

In search of a value-free label for PSE, I was much enlightened by an article written by Dennis Cokely on the subject. In the article, Cokely says that no single satisfactory definition of the phenomenon called "pidgin" has yet emerged from the field of linguistics; however there are specific preconditions necessary for a pidgin to develop. He lists the preconditions, analyzes their relevance for ASL, and concludes that, ". . . none of the preconditions has been sufficiently met to allow a pidgin to develop." (Cokely, 1983, p.7)

If what we have been calling a pidgin is not a true pidgin, because the necessary preconditions for its development are not present, then what is it? Cokely answers ". . . that what has been called Pidgin Sign English is in fact a product of the linguistic accommodations made by deaf and hearing people interacting with the other group." (Cokely, 1983, p.10) I shifted then from "PSE" to "a product of linguistic accommodations" in search of a more acceptable label, but that seemed a bit vague, indistinct, and much too cumbersome to serve as a name.

Cokely defines this "product" as a "register," which he says ". . . is a particular way of using a language in a particular situation." (Cokely, 1983, p.9) When ASL is used in certain settings such as a classroom, a church or temple, a professional technical gathering, a sporting event, a play, a deaf club, etc., it accommodates itself to the situation, and the product is a register.

If PSE is a register, what kind of register is it and how did it come about? Cokely describes the process by which the PSE register evolved.

> "For example, a hearing person beginning to sign may initially rely upon the syntax of English, and so produce more English-like signing; then, gaining more proficiency in ASL, will rely less on the native language but will overgeneralize ASL syntactic features, producing more ASL-like but still not native signing. Whether the person stops learning there (fossilizes) or goes on to gain native-like competence in ASL depends upon the extent to which the individual is accepted by and acculturated into the target society, the Deaf community." (Cokely, 1983, p.14)

PSE is the product of hearing people who have either "fossilized," or have not been accepted and acculturated into the deaf community. Cokely calls this product a foreigner talk register. Cokely goes on to describe in more detail how this foreigner talk register happens.

"One more point worth considering is that the foreigner talk register of ASL also functions as the language model the hearing learner is most likely to be exposed to. Hence, the model that learners are most often striving to emulate is actually different from the standard registers of the target language that they suppose they are learning. Because the foreigner talk register is used when the learner is perceived as an "outsider" (whether because introduced as hearing or because of attempts to use ASL), it becomes extremely difficult for the learner to gain exposure to the norms of the target language." (Cokely, 1983, p.19)

Lest deaf people who prefer to use PSE be insulted, or transliterators of PSE feel their abilities to be impugned, I prefer not to relabel PSE as a "foreigner talk register." My preference is to call it simply an English-like register, a label unencumbered with any value judgment of the user's skill or choice.

I believe Cokely has effectively argued that there is no such thing as a true pidgin as far as the ASL-English situation is concerned. I propose we cease to refer to the phenomenon as "PSE," and instead call it "an English-like register of ASL" ("ERA" for short?). My reasons are that "pidgin" sounds condescending, and the reality of PSE's existence is at best questionable.

Furthermore, we will, by so doing, take one more step towards ridding our nomenclature of labels that are misleading. The next step is to get rid of the term, "transliterate."

A transliteration is the writing or spelling of one language in the alphabetic characters or symbols of another language. An example of this is the writing of Hebrew in the English alphabet so that those unable to read Hebrew can pronounce it. Even if one fingerspelled all the spoken words, it would not be transliterating because one would still be using the English alphabet.

We should cease to talk of transliterating (which we do not do) into PSE (whose existence is questionable), and rather speak of the act as interpreting into an English-like register of ASL. We would, by so doing, remove the implication that ASL is a language limited to social, non-technical, non-professional discourse. If ASL is a legitimate language, as we claim, then it has in common with all languages the characteristic of more than a single register.

Another unfortunate fallout occasioned by our use of the PSE label is that we have unwittingly coerced many deaf people into proclaiming that they prefer PSE to ASL, even when they converse among themselves. We have created the illusion that they do not know or use ASL. What we have done is to refuse to recognize intracultural differences and preferences within the deaf community. We must accept with alacrity that ASL has various registers and that deaf people prefer one register to another at various times and occasions, and we must have the good sense to know which register is appropriate for an interpretation.

What Happens When There is No Stated Philosophy

We who founded RID knew who we were: educators, vocational rehabilitation workers, deaf leaders, deaf workers, religious workers, and interpreters who worked at some job and interpreted, when available, for free. We all had jobs that were clearly defined, so we knew what was expected of us. There was no confusion about our purpose and objective: to provide interpretation services to deaf people. Furthermore, most of us had grown up in close contact with deaf people.

It is fair to say that a majority, if not all of us, took the physical disability view of deafness. It was, after all, if not the only view extant at that time, certainly the overwhelmingly predominant one. It never occurred to us that there might be an alternative perspective. Because there was no confusion about who we were and what we did, and because we were of like mind in our attitude toward deaf people, we felt no need for a statement of philosophy to guide us.

As the years passed the membership of RID changed dramatically. It slowly evolved into an organization of people whose primary work was interpretation. These people came from backgrounds where they experienced little, if any, contact with deaf people prior to learning ASL. Having had little exposure to the physical disability perspective, they carried no brief for it, and indeed had few prejudices one way or another toward deaf people.

The influx of people from outside the world of deafness, who looked upon deafness with unbiased eyes, challenged the attitudes, values, and beliefs of those of us who had labored for many years in the field. They gravitated toward the sociolinguistic view of deafness and questioned RID's positions. Naturally there was resentment which erupted often in heated debates. The most intense debate has been with regard to oral interpreting.

There was no question in the minds of the founders of RID that oral interpretation was a needed service and that it fell within the purview of RID's jurisdiction. This is clearly seen in the last paragraph of the quote on page 14:

> *"The method of interpreting or translating may be manual and/or oral."*

Further evidence of this attitude is provided in the manual produced at the Maine Workshop. One section with regard to training interpreters is entitled, "Interpreting for the Orally Oriented Deaf." No one questioned the need for oral interpretation, nor the fact that interpreters ought to receive training in this skill.

Oral interpretation did not, indeed could not, become an issue until there were sufficient numbers within RID's membership who viewed interpreting as a strictly defined operation involving two languages. These were the people mentioned above who came from interpreter training programs, or from linguistic backgrounds. They saw that oral interpretation was not interpretation at all since only one language was involved.

The fact that the controversy arose at all is indicative of two important changes that were evolving within RID. First, ASL was being recognized as a language and interpretation involved the two languages, English and ASL. Second, the physical disability view of deafness, which had geared our thinking along the lines of social service, was giving way to the sociolinguistic view, which guided our thinking towards the professionalization of interpretation. Conflict was inevitable and, though it has produced pain, it has been healthy. Growth does not occur without change, and change, especially of attitudes, is usually painful.

The controversy began to bubble to the surface sometime during the late seventies. The Council on Education of the Deaf (CED) made the following resolution in 1979:

"CED views the role of Oral Interpreter as a necessary adjunct to equal opportunity for all hearing impaired individuals (deaf and hard of hearing) and recommends that agencies involved with the provision of or training or certification of Simultaneous or Manual Interpreters of the Deaf consider the establishment of guidelines, competencies and criteria for certification of Oral Interpreters as soon as practicable." (Council on Education for the Deaf)

36

In a later issue of *VIEWS*, Robert Ingram stated the opposite position:

"I do not question the right of deaf persons to communicate orally or to employ the services of communications specialists who are more easily lipread. I have performed such duties myself. However, interpreting always involves two languages, and 'oral interpreting' involves only one. Psycholinguists have long studied the process of repeating a language simultaneously as it is heard and have labeled the process 'shadowing'... Another major question which has not yet been resolved to my satisfaction is whether such evaluation and certification is a reasonable project for the R.I.D. to sponsor. It may be that such a project is best left to the Alexander Graham Bell Association for the Deaf with technical assistance provided by the R.I.D." (Ingram)

And thus the battle was joined.

Susan D. Fischer took issue with Ingram's position:

"Ingram's third question: Is there such a thing as oral interpreting? is perhaps the most disturbing since it shows a misunderstanding of interpreting in general, and oral interpreting in particular. A good interpreter adjusts his/her signing along the continuum between MCE and ASL to reflect the changing needs of the text, the setting, and the audience. Thus, a skilled interpreter must be able both to "interpret," i.e., translate between English and ASL, and to "transliterate," i.e., transfer one modality of English into another. If most interpreters tend to "transliterate" rather than "interpret" most of the time, it may be because this is the most appropriate thing to do—for example, if one must change a lecturer's spoken English into signing which will be comprehensible to a mixed group of native and non-native signers. Thus, no matter what Ingram's personal opinions are, it is already both explicitly and implicitly RID policy to, when appropriate, change spoken English into a form of English which is readily apprehended visually. Oral interpreting can be seen as an *extension*, not a contradiction, of this policy. Furthermore, oral interpreting does not consist merely of mouthing everything the speaker says; rather, as Ingram himself would probably admit, it involves the complex skill of paraphrasing where necessary to make English more visually accessible to the oral deaf person." (Fischer)

In order to understand better the oral interpreter certification controversy, we need to pause here and examine the historical oral-manual controversy which has raged in the field of education since the late eighteenth century. I do not intend to plow once more those weary, oft tilled furrows of barren land upon which nothing but weeds will take root. Others have put the case more eloquently than I can as to the insidious, debilitating effects of outlawing ASL in the education of deaf people. I intend, rather, to focus on some of the dynamics of the controversy in order to provide an understanding of how it has affected our profession of interpreting.

I referred earlier to Harlan Lane's book as being a history of how the majority cannot abide differences within its society and must act to remove those differences by assimilation and integration. Xenophobia, the fear of anything foreign or strange, runs deep in the well springs of all human societies, and though it may appear extreme to classify the historical antipathy against ASL as xenophobia, it must be seen as a manifestation of it in order for us to appreciate the power of the oral argument.

Few of us relish classification as different, as being an outsider, a non-conformist, a person who will not go along with the crowd. The potency of peer pressure to be like everyone else is a reminder of how irresistible the strength of this facet of xenophobia is. The need to be like everyone else makes the oral argument much easier to sell than the manual one, and accounts for the success the oralists have had over the years. Though the failure of the oral approach has been demonstrated and documented time and again, it has lost little of its appeal to the unsuspecting public, because it caters to that fear we have of the alien thing.

The oral argument prevailed for so long because it fueled society's fear that if ASL be accorded its due place, deaf people would be empowered to determine their own destinies, and thus set themselves apart from the rest of us in some arcane establishment of their own, unintelligible to society at large. Not only have deaf people had to struggle against the xenophobia of hearing people, but also they had to engage in a struggle to wrest power from hearing people. It was, and still is, in the final analysis, a power struggle as to who had the greater right to establish the rules of the game. Oral interpretation was far less an issue about needed services than it was one of who decided what.

The last two decades have witnessed an inexorable erosion of the power base of the oral establishment. The recognition of ASL as a language, the deaf culture movement, demonstrations by deaf students and by deaf actors, the Total Communication movement, and the attacks against the indiscriminate mainstreaming of deaf children all served notice that the deaf community was on the move to gain the reins of power to determine what is best for them. Oralism was besieged from all quarters; its long standing dominion over deaf people was crumbling; its legitimacy as a knowledgeable, influential force was being questioned; its pervasive doctrine was on the wane. It was in the throes of a desperate struggle to regain its former prominence.

The oral establishment chose as one path back to its position of eminence that which would seemingly ally itself with ASL. If it could succeed in becoming part and parcel of the one institution that stands taller than any other in the promotion of ASL, it would have taken a giant step toward its re-empowerment. Recognition by RID would have infused tremendous energy into its efforts to regain its previous status.

The first effort to change the name of RID was made as an outcome of this controversy. The proposed name was the National Association of Sign Language Interpreters, with the less than subtle intention of excluding oral interpreters. But, in the November 1980 meeting of the board, the proposed name change was rejected. The following rationale was offered:

> "The historical intention has been to serve all deaf people. The organization is currently recognized as the RID and has been written into Federal legislation. A name change would discriminate against deaf persons who choose to utilize various modes of communication." (Fall Board Meeting—Dallas, Tex.)*

There is a continuing effort to change RID's name, but it springs from an entirely different motivation than that of 1980. The rationale is that we are not interpreters for deaf people only, but for hearing people as well. To continue to label ourselves as, "interpreters for the deaf," perpetuates the emphasis on the physical disability and promotes a patronizing attitude. The amount of sentiment for a name change, though not yet large enough to effect the change, signals a significant shift from the physical disability to the sociolinguistic orientation.

If there had been a statement of philosophy from the beginning, the oral interpreter controversy would still have arisen. It is inevitable

---

*It should be remembered that the board had all authority to make decisions for the organization and resolutions were not subject to a referendum.

that controversial issues arise as an organization evolves to meet new circumstances and new ideas. What a statement might have averted, or at least minimized, was the feeling that the arguments were directed at specific individuals. People were accused of ulterior motives, unprofessional behavior, and general mischief making. The focus shifted from the issue to personalities, largely because the issue was not grounded in a cogent statement of what RID believed in.

The oral interpreter controversy is a classic example of a dialectic conflict in which a thesis is challenged by an antithesis and from this evolves a synthesis. It is the normal progression of human activity. We do not yet know what the synthesis will be, but it ought to be stated in written form as our philosophy. Perhaps, then, when a future antithesis arises to contest it, as it surely will, the debates can be calmer, more rational, and focused on ideas, not personalities. In the meantime we will have rid ourselves of the miasma that surrounds our uncertainty of who we are and what we do.

Twenty-Five Years Later

We started out as a loose and widely scattered band of people who worked at various careers and did interpretation on the side, usually for free. We became a more tightly knit group, hired a full-time executive director, established a home office, and began to have biennial conventions. Then we lost a lot of ground: we ran out of money, had no executive director nor home office for a period of time. During this period, we began the process of rejuvenation: we managed to hire an executive director, set up a home office, draw up new bylaws which democratized the organization and provided a new framework for us to move ahead in a more orderly fashion.

At the twenty-fifth anniversary convention in El Paso, Texas, 1989, several resolutions were passed which will have a profound impact on our organization. One of them dealt with recertification. At the St. Paul Convention, 1987, a resolution was passed that requires all certified members to be recertified through the new certification system. At the El Paso Convention a motion to rescind the St. Paul motion was narrowly defeated. There was, and still is, much disagreement among the membership about this issue. Many certified interpreters have said they will not seek recertification. If they follow through with their decision, they will presumably also withdraw from membership in RID. It remains to be seen how many members will pursue this course, and how it will affect the organization.

Another motion passed at El Paso had to do with dual membership. The motion requires that all members of local affiliates must also be members of RID in order to vote on actions to be taken by the affiliates. Several affiliate presidents proclaimed that they would lose many if not a majority of their members because of this ruling. If such transpires, this too could alter the character of our organization.

Other actions taken at El Paso affect the dues structure for associate members (a one-time 10% increase), and the fees for taking the new certification test. These actions might also reduce the number of members in the associate and certified categories.

Opinions were expressed at El Paso that reflected two attitudes toward the possible departure of a large number of members. One attitude was that such an outcome would make RID less representative of the field of interpretation, and thus set us back once more. The other attitude was that RID would lose only such members who are not committed to the professionalization of interpretation and will be the healthier for it. At this writing it is not possible to predict what effects these motions will have upon RID, but one way or the other, there will be aftershocks.

I see this as further proof that we are still in search of our identity. We have not yet made up our minds whether we are a social service organization, or an organization devoted strictly to the field of interpretation. The trend, in my view, seems to be toward the latter position. If such is the case, there will no doubt be some shrinkage in the number of members, but this need not portend the demise of RID, nor even its ability to represent the field of interpretation. I see it as a phase that we must pass through in order to define with greater precision who we are and what we do. The outcome will, I think, improve the rapport with our clients and the quality of service they can expect from us.

It is a mistake for an individual or an organization to attempt to be all things to all people. As a group, we must agree that we provide specified services in clearly defined ways, and that if other services are needed, other organizations must provide them. I further believe this will not be accomplished without a well articulated philosophy to guide us.

CERTIFICATION

Beginnings

The fact that certification is only alluded to in the minutes of the organization meeting which founded RID is indicative of the low priority it held in our agenda of things that needed to be done. The entry reads: "The idea of an accreditation program was also brought up but if anything is to be done on this it will have to be in the future." (Minutes of Organizational Meeting, p.5) The reference might have been to training programs, or to interpreters themselves, but whichever it was, there was no pressing mandate for it.

Since one of the major reasons for establishing RID was to supply consumers with a registry of competent interpreters, it might seem odd that we made no strong recommendations for action that would result in an instrument to measure competency. It can be partly explained by saying that most of us were not oriented to look at interpreting from a scientific point of view, a condition of thinking that is still all too prevalent today.

For several years one established one's claim to competency and to be placed on the registry by securing the signatures of two RID members to support the claim. This was not a totally invalid way to assess competency since most of the members were skilled interpreters and quite adept at spotting other skilled interpreters, or they were consumers who were sophisticated at identification of skilled interpreters. As people rapidly gained entrance to RID, however, the number of interpreters with minimal skills increased because they in turn supported the acceptance of still more such interpreters until the registry became highly suspect.

42

We were not totally naive about this hearsay method of attesting one's credentials, just slow to do anything about it. In January of 1965 we held the Follow-Up Workshop on Interpreting for the Deaf at which we gave some serious thought to certification. Dr. William E. Kendall, vice-president, The Psychological Corporation, was invited to speak on the subject. He and his company were professional developers of certification programs. He provided us with these excellent guidelines:

"What are the characteristics of an adequate licensing or certification examination? I like to think of seven requirements which must be met.

(1) An adequate examination must cover the areas of required knowledge and skill. This means that through research and consultation with experts in the field areas of required knowledge and skill are determined. Care must be exercised in setting forth these areas so that 'must know,' 'should know,' and 'would be nice to know' areas can be identified and material from the latter two areas minimized or eliminated.

(2) An adequate examination must be of a level of difficulty such that a passing score will represent, at a minimum, a capable, journeyman level of knowledge and skill in the field. A licensing or certification examination normally marks the end of formal training in a field, it represents the last check which a regulatory body makes of an individual's skill or knowledge in a field. Thus, the examination serves as one criterion in judging the individual's competence to offer his services to the public. This means that the difficulty level of the examination must be such as to provide assurance that the individual possesses at least a minimum level of required knowledge and skill.

(3) An adequate examination must be reliable and must sample the required knowledge and skill thoroughly to assure that neither 'good luck' or 'bad luck' plays a part in determining the score obtained. It is obvious that if an entire examination were to consist of but one question drawn from an infinite universe of possible questions, differences in emphasis while preparing for the examination might result in either a perfect score or a zero score on the part of an otherwise well trained and generally well prepared candidate.

(4) An adequate examination must be secure so that the person taking it, although properly forewarned as to the areas covered, can not have had access to the particular questions. While it is perfectly proper for a candidate to know what areas are to be covered in an examination and to be aware of the item types employed, an examination ceases to be a valid measure of knowledge and skill when it has been compromised.

(5) An adequate examination must be administered in such a way that each candidate has a fair and equal opportunity to display his knowledge or skill without the help of books or of other persons. A test administration procedure that contains no positive safeguards against cribbing, coaching or other unauthorized assistance tends to encourage 'little' breaches of test security that soon invalidate the test as a measure of knowledge or skill.

(6) An adequate examination must be scored accurately and impartially so that no additional elements of error or chance are introduced. Unless the scoring or evaluation procedure is so designed as to reflect accurately in the scores obtained the relative amounts of knowledge or skill possessed by candidates, the examination grade is of little real value for certification purposes.

(7) An adequate examination, finally, must be efficient, requiring a minimum amount of time and expense for the candidate, be easy to administer and simple and inexpensive to score." (Taylor, p.24-25)

Dr. Kendall closed with the following statement.

"What are the next steps? In developing other examinations, I have followed this general outline: research on 'must know,' development of blue print, development of item prototypes, pretest of candidate populations, development of norms and standards, preparation of final forms of the examination for field use." (Taylor, p.26)

He made it abundantly clear that much research must precede any attempt to construct an instrument for certifying competency.

In the final report of the proceedings of the workshop, the following appears:

"The following points were accepted as being the consensus of opinion of the participants at this workshop concerning examination and certification of interpreters:

1. The Executive Board of the Registry of Interpreters for the Deaf shall establish a board of examiners.
2. The board of examiners shall determine the minimal examination requirements.
3. The paper *The Characteristics of an Adequate Certification or Licensing Examination Program* presented by William E. Kendall, Ph.D., Vice-President, The Psychological Corporation, should provide the guidelines for the establishment of the Registry of Interpreters for the Deaf as a certifying organization.
4. Among those serving on the examining board, there shall be one officer from the Registry of Interpreters for the Deaf and one deaf person.
5. The use of films and tapes in examining candidates for certification are recommended." (Taylor, p.22)

The only action taken on these recommendations was to set up nine boards of examiners around the country as recommended above. It is unclear from the literature, or from my memory, exactly what these boards did, but they were probably meant to be in place, ready to operate whenever a certification examination became a reality.

At the workshop held in San Francisco in July of 1966, some of us decided to make one more attempt to get certification started on the right foot.

"The following resolution was the result of a committee from the group and based on the area felt to be one of the most critical:

3. Whereas R.I.D. has had a Steering Committee for Development for certification procedures.

Therefore be it resolved that the R.I.D. establish a committee to approach an appropriate collegiate institution to prepare a proposal for a research and demonstration grant which shall have as its purpose the development of certification standards and procedures.

This grant proposal shall include provision for the:

1. Construction and validation of instruments for the measurement of interpretive competency;
2. Standardization of procedures for administration, scoring and evaluation." (*A Workshop to Activate Interpreting Services for Deaf People*, p.30)

The committee that made the recommendation suggested that the lack of funds for the project could be surmounted by applying, through a university, for a grant. No action, however, was ever taken.

Our failure to act was due to the fact that RID was made up of members scattered across the country with practically no contact with each other. We had not yet begun to have national conventions, so there was no opportunity to marshal support for the project. It was difficult to inform the members of the proposed action, and even more difficult to get back from them a consensus of what they wanted. Even if such had been feasible, final authority for action rested with the board, and the board did not see fit, for whatever reasons, to take action.

The first newsletter sent out in November of 1967 by Pimentel, as the new executive director, mentions that RID is exploring with Captioned Films for the Deaf the possibility of developing standardized testing materials for certification. At that time, RID was operating under the grant mentioned earlier from VRA, and possibly some funds were available to initiate the project. I have found no evidence, however, that anything came of the exploration with Captioned Films for the Deaf.

First Steps

When NAD applied to VRA in 1967 for a grant to set up a home office for RID with a full-time staff, the grant proposal listed six goals:

a. Preparing and administering examinations to determine competency of prospective members of the Registry;
b. Publicizing the existence of the Registry and its services;
c. Recruiting of interpreting personnel in such areas as circumstances dictate;

    d.   Encouraging research conducive to improvement and expansion of interpretation services for the deaf;

    e.   Preparing standards of performance and guidelines for interpreters, examiners, and training personnel;

    f.   Developing training programs and procedures to ensure a constant and expanding supply of qualified interpreters. (*Application for Research or Demonstration Grant*, p.6)

Inasmuch as certification was listed in first position, we may assume it was to have had priority over the other goals. After five years, however, no such system was in place. In a personal conversation, Carl Kirchner, president of RID in 1972 when the grant ended, informed me that VRA exerted pressure on RID to get a certification system set up immediately. Again, expediency became the motive for the system.

As activity suddenly accelerated, it seemed the wisest course to adopt a system that was already functioning.

"As the five year grant ran out it became more and more evident that an evaluation system for the increasing number of interpreters was necessary. Several things had occurred during these years which pointed to this fact. A workshop, sponsored by the Social and Rehabilitation Services Department in 1966 in California mandated that the R.I.D. Board begin to explore evaluation and certification of interpreters. From 1968-1972 the Texas Society of Interpreters for the Deaf implemented an evaluation system for interpreters in Texas. In 1972 at the second R.I.D. convention the decision was made to conduct a national evaluation of interpreters. In order to fund this decision several of the staff members of the National Office were terminated and full efforts were directed to the development of the evaluation of interpreters. The Southern California R.I.D. utilized, modified and expanded the evaluation information and procedures obtained from the Texas chapter. The evaluation model of the Southern California R.I.D. chapter operated for two years as a pilot project for the R.I.D. from 1970-72." ("RID Enters New Decade")

 In October of 1972 a workshop was held in Memphis, Tennessee, to launch the certification system. Each local chapter was asked to send its best interpreter to be tested; these individuals then received instruction on conducting tests in their local areas.

In view of the fact that the tests had not been scientifically developed and subjected to rigorous field testing, it is surprising that the certification system worked at all. There were, to be sure, complaints about the test materials, and the rating system. Accusations of bias against a candidate by local evaluators were not uncommon. Some local evaluation teams quickly gained a reputation of being more strict than others, and it was not unusual for candidates to take the test in another area where the team was known to score more liberally. It was, however, the best that we could do, given the circumstances.

We lived with the system for fifteen years before a new one was instituted. In 1986, RID received a grant from the Fund for the Improvement of Post Secondary Education (FIPSE) to develop, validate, and make reliable a new certification examination. A full-time administrator was brought in to oversee the project. In 1987, the new test was started and is the one under which we now operate.

We have had an unfortunate history with regard to research. The usual excuse is that there was insufficient funding, but I am of the opinion that a more accurate explanation lies in a basic mistrust of the value of research. We have heard of and read about study after study whose findings were suspect, of researchers who have altered data to support their own biases, of trivial research to fulfill Ph.D. requirements; and these investigations have caused us to cast a jaundiced eye at research in general. Add to this the skepticism that runs through the American character of the halls of academe from which emerge ivory-tower, egg-headed thinking. We are proud of our practical, pragmatic approach to solving problems and thus place little value on theoretical endeavors.

Our history, with regard to certification, has been one of trial and error, hit or miss, rather than one based on research. We have measured skills, attitudes, and various other attributes without first discovering whether they are relevant, and if they are, whether we can measure them at all, and finally whether the instrument we are using will in fact measure them. Our first set of tests used to certify interpreters was a classic example of this approach. It was totally devoid of any scientific underpinning, and we are still paying for our mistake.

Had we not ignored Dr. Kendall's program in 1965, we would not have found it imperative to spend great sums of money and energy to create a new set of tests in 1987. It became necessary to make this investment because the first set simply did not do what it was intended to do. My certification became suspect because too many unqualified interpreters were certified. I do not begrudge spending the time, energy, and money to take the new tests because I want my certification to mean something. I am annoyed only because we failed to do it right the first time.

We need a great deal more research to aid us in devising training programs. How can we prepare interpreters for their work when we know so little about what skills are needed? Even if we knew that much, how can we know the best ways to develop those skills, without research? Without a body of knowledge supported by research and confirmed by practice, we will continue to fall short of the professionalization we seek in our field.

We need to affirm the indispensability of research by seeking grants for it, by approaching scientists and institutions with projects, and, most of all, by developing a healthier respect for it than we have had in the past. We recognize that researchers do err, but that does not justify a resistant attitude toward all research. We need to effect a happy marriage between research and practical experience so that we, and our consumers, can be assured that we have done all we can to provide the best service possible.

What Certification Means

Like the mist that veils the fabled entrance of Shangri-La, a mystique has grown up about the meaning of certification that shields reality from our eyes, and clouds our minds as to the meaning of certification. We have made of it something it was never intended to be, indeed, can never be, a panacea for our ills. We seem to believe that if only we can vaccinate interpreters with the serum of certification, they will be forever immune to errors, bad judgement, poor signing, and lapses of competency.

Webster's *New World Dictionary, Second College Edition* defines *competent* as, "(1) well qualified; capable; fit (2) sufficient; adequate (3) permissible or properly belonging (4) Law legally qualified, authorized, or fit." There is not even a hint that competency equals perfection. RID certification may be compared to an academic diploma or degree which vouches that the bearer has demonstrated a command of certain knowledge and skills. It does not guarantee possession of knowledge and skills that can be obtained only through continued advanced study, application, experience and wisdom.

Neumann Solow says that certification is

". . .merely the stamp of approval of basic skills. It indicates the basic ability to serve in the capacity of a sign language interpreter. There is no guarantee that the interpreter who receives his or her certification can adequately serve in every situation he or she encounters, but certification implies that he or she can serve in almost any situation. Certification is like getting a driver's license. Just as the driver's license gives the driver the right to drive on our streets and certifies basic competency behind the wheel, so RID certification establishes the basic competency of the sign language interpreter to interpret in most situations. It does not distinguish between various levels of interpreters, just as a driver's license does not qualify anyone for the 'Indy 500.' However, anyone who drives in the Indy 500 does first need to have a driver's license." (Neumann Solow, p.84-85)

Our task is first to make certain we have a clear understanding of the basic competency warranted by RID certification, which should be spelled out in our philosophy, and then to convey that understanding to our consumers. I shall not attempt to delineate the specifics of basic competency, that is for those who write our philosophy, but I shall suggest some of the components that should be covered.

A certified interpreter must be one who has basic competency at a specified level of ASL fluency, has amassed a specified number of hours of supervised practicum, has a specified level of knowledge of linguistics and theory of interpretation, and has attained a specified level of knowledge of deaf culture, including its history. A certified interpreter has demonstrated her/his knowledge, experience, and abilities in the above areas, through written and performance examinations to the satisfaction of RID.

We must constantly keep in mind that certification means basic competency, not advanced expertise. When interpreters, like physicians and lawyers complete their schooling, receive their certificates/ licenses, and begin to practice, they are not expected to be as proficient as they will become after years of experience. As they grow in knowledge and experience, some will excel, most will be adequate, and some will fall by the wayside. Success will depend on many factors, one of which is talent. Nature does not distribute talent equally. Those with more talent, drive, dedication, and tenacity will most likely be the ones to rise above the others and be perceived as the best. All will be certified, but only a few will be superior.

Somehow, we have failed to convey to our consumers a clear understanding of what RID certification means. As a result, consumers have unrealistic expectations of RID certified interpreters. Consumers have come to expect all certified interpreters to be equal in their abilities and to operate at the highest level of expertise. Instead of competency analogous to a B.A. degree, consumers expect competency represented by a Ph.D., *magna cum laude*.

Consumers tend to base their acceptance or rejection of interpreters upon two factors: skill and personality. If the signing is clear, easily understood, and meaningful, the interpreter is adjudged to be skillful. Unfortunately, if the personality of the interpreter is perceived to be unattractive, a concept too subjective to be further defined, the interpreter will not be adjudged to be competent.

Overall, personality and specific character traits exert a powerful impact upon the consumer's perception of an interpreter's competency. It is regrettable that such intangible subtleties often decide whether the consumer will like or dislike an interpreter, but it is a fact we must live with. It would be folly to imagine we could transform personalities, even if we knew what traits are desirable to instill. Training programs cannot alter personalities, and certification does not measure their attractability quotient. We are left with no alternative save that of explaining to consumers that they must not confuse competency with such things as attractiveness, likeability, warmth, friendliness and any other traits that might come to mind.

One further point with regard to any certification system must be considered: no matter how scientifically developed, administered, and scored, some incompetent interpreters will manage to pass. We must expect this to happen, but let us not condemn a system for being less than perfect.

Recertification

As I mentioned earlier, the issue of recertification has been a hotly debated one, and has caused no little division among the membership. Although the motion in El Paso to rescind the St. Paul motion failed to carry (p.37) it was a close vote and the issue may not yet be settled. The explanation for resistance to recertification lies in the checkered history of RID certification procedures.

When we first began to certify members in 1972, certificates were good for only five years, at which time one had to be recertified.

"When the time came for the first group of expired certificate holders to be recertified, RID was not prepared to re-evaluate them and began a long succession of extending certification expiration dates which has continued to the present." (Report by the Ad Hoc Committee on Recertification and Maintenance, p.3)

Eventually it was decided that those whose certificates had expired could re-take the same test under which they were certified, which had been modified with new materials. Those who chose to do this were promised that they would not have to be recertified again.

In the late seventies and early eighties, a new test was devised for interpreters to be recognized at a higher level of performance than the regular test. Those who passed this test received Master Comprehensive Skills Certificates (MCSC). They too were promised that they would not have to be recertified again.

In both cases, the recertified CSC's, and the MCSC's, it was understood that to continue to keep their certification valid, they would have to follow a maintenance program.

"This maintenance program would grant credits for professional development ensuring that interpreters would keep up-to-date with knowledge of the profession. This program was begun but never successfully implemented and both re-evaluation exams were suspended by RID after a short period with only a few interpreters recertified." (ibid., p.4)

In November 1982, the board decided to discontinue the MCSC, along with several other categories. The rationale given was:

"The RID is currently doing evaluations at a loss. The present financial constrains (sic) of the organization demand that only the most basic certificates be awarded." ("Board of Directors Action, 1982")

At the time, RID offered ten different certificates, so it is not unreasonable to assume there were not funds to continue the operation.

One year later, the board decided to discontinue the Certification Maintenance Program (CMP). Four reasons were given. The first was that the CMP lacked the mechanism to document and verify the variety of continuing education units turned in by members. Second, the CMP lacked a way to document hours of interpretation reported. Third, the CMP lacked a system for maintaining the certified status of interpreters who did not work regularly or at all. Fourth, it was felt that the new evaluation system, which was anticipated to appear shortly, would change the whole approach of the CMP. ("RID Board of Directors Meeting," 1983)

The failure to continue recertification of CSC's, to award MCSC's, and to implement the CMP did not invalidate the promises made, and the reason recertification under the current program is resisted is because of those promises. Although I sympathize with those to whom promises were given, I believe it is in their best interest, the best interest of the profession and the consumer that they do become recertified under the current system. I have several reasons for this belief.

The content of the current test is much more realistic in terms of interpretation settings than was the former test. It gives a better measure of the interpreter's ability to function in a variety of settings.

The evaluation of the interpreter's performance is more objective than the former test. The interpreter's performance is compared to what the profession as a whole deems is acceptable or unacceptable, and not subject to local norms which varied enormously under the former system.

Because of the national norm, we have a more accurate baseline measure of our skills. We know more precisely where we stand with regard to all other certified interpreters. This also provides us with a common bond that fosters a spirit of unity and cooperation.

Finally, it is a demonstration of our commitment to professionalization. By taking the test we proclaim our determination to maintain the highest standards for ourselves. We also set an example for the young interpreters entering the field. How can we in good conscience encourage them to become certified if we refuse to do so?

The Next Step

The enormous expenditure of resources and time over the last seventeen years could easily lead one to conclude that the certification of interpreters is RID's *raison d'etre*. It is time, now that our new certification procedure is in place and functioning, to consider turning this responsibility over to an independent agency.

A reasonable alternative to the present situation would be to contract with an agency that specializes in devising, administering, and scoring examinations for professional organizations to do the work for us. As time goes on, some modifications in the examination will be necessary, and RID would supply the agency with an advisory board to improve and update the procedure. The agency would turn over to RID its data, and RID would then issue certificates.

Two important benefits would accrue to us all under some such arrangement as that described above. First, RID would have no vested interest in the outcome, thus certification would be placed on a far more objective footing. Second, the home office staff and local affiliate personnel would be freed up to attend to what ought to be the main business of RID, fostering the professional growth of us all.

Revenues ought to be spent on the development of materials to be used in conferences, workshops, and seminars to help interpreters improve their skills. Videotapes and computer programs need to be developed for interpreters to continue their education in groups, or alone through home study programs. The publication arm needs to be expanded to provide more literature for us and consumers, as well as to raise more funds. A service whereby an interpreter may send in a videotape of her/his performance to be critiqued should be set up. RID needs to work with the Conference of Interpreter Trainers to develop and revise curricula. RID needs to develop consumer education programs. These are examples of things we can do once we cease to siphon off personnel and funds to support the certification program.

A Trend

The historical evolution of professional certification in the United States has followed a course of beginning as a national certification, then metamorphosing into state and local certification or licensing. We need look no further than the certification of teachers of deaf children for a classic illustration of this process.

When schools for deaf children were first established, states did not certify the teachers. The Conference of Executives of American Schools for the Deaf (CEASD) issued certificates to graduates of programs that trained teachers of deaf children. Even after states instituted their own certification programs, the CEASD certificate was widely accepted in lieu of state certification, or as a provisional certificate.

In the mid sixties, the Council on Education of the Deaf (CED) took over the certification of teachers from the CEASD. Today a few states accept CED certification as sufficient, but most require their own certification, even though, in the opinion of many people, CED requirements for certification are more rigorous than many states' requirements.

It is quite likely that certification of interpreters will follow the same path. Already there are stirrings in a few states toward this end. Great care must be exercised in the coming years not to put ourselves in the position of opposing state certification. To the contrary, RID ought to assist in the transition whenever it occurs.

The years of expertise in certifying interpreters accumulated by RID ought to be made available to a state in order to help it avoid the pitfalls we experienced. RID, through its national staff and local affiliate personnel, in concert with the state chapter of NAD, can present to the proper state agency responsible for certification and licensure a proposal for certifying interpreters and a package of already prepared examinations. We would be acting in the best interests of consumers by protecting them from the debacles that too often ensue when purposeful action is forfeited for the sake of expediency.

If certification becomes less the responsibility of RID, and more the function of states, it will present a true measure of professionalism. No longer will we be motivated to get RID certification just so we can work, but rather as a way to express our dedication to our profession. RID certification will not be merely a union card for employment, but rather a badge of distinction, the stamp of approval from our peers. We will become members of RID in order to promote our growth in professional knowledge and skills, and to enhance the growth of the profession itself. It will mark our maturity, our coming of age.

TRAINING

In the beginning there was only the Watch And Do Likewise University. The preparatory program took place in our homes with our parents as tutors. Our advanced training consisted of watching experienced interpreters at work, then trying to imitate them. Our diplomas were awarded to us by the deaf community in the form of praise and requests for our services. Watch And Do Likewise University had few graduates, far too few to fulfill all the requests that came in, but those who did graduate were first-class interpreters.

With the coming of RID, old WADLU began to fade into the background. People began to believe there was a better way to increase the supply of competent interpreters with a higher percentage of success. The quality of skill may not have been significantly increased with this new movement, but the quantity certainly was. I do not intend any disparagement toward those who have joined our ranks via routes other than that of old WADLU, but rather I mean for us to recognize the products of WADLU as deserving honor and respect from us, despite their lack of formal training.

I have observed that young interpreters today are often seized with panic when they embark on their maiden assignments, especially when they do their first platform interpretation. Yet, they have had the benefit of formal training with hours of supervised trial and error efforts in the relative safety of the classroom. Imagine how much more terrified we, who had not had that training, were when we began. It was a shattering experience that only the bold and hardy survived.

I am gratified that today interpreters do not have to face the ordeal of interpreting with no prior structured preparation to equip them. Anyone today who is interested in becoming an interpreter does not have to look far from home to find an interpreter training program (ITP), for they are numerous. They are not all equal in quality, of course, but neither are schools, colleges, and universities all equal in the quality of education and training they provide. The student of superior ability will rise above her/his institution and excel in spite of mediocre programs.

As was said earlier, one of the major purposes for the founding of RID was to train interpreters. The Maine Workshop was convened specifically to address that need. Until 1979, RID assumed primary responsibility for the ITP's, but that amounted to little more than encouragement and moral support. Few individuals had an inkling of how to go about training interpreters. How could they? There were no programs through which they could have learned how to train interpreters. Everyone was pretty much on their own. There was no organization to accredit ITP's, so the quality of a program depended upon the experience, skill, and inventiveness of those who ran it.

The Vocational Rehabilitation Act of 1973 provided grants to set up ITP's. Six institutions were chosen to receive the grants (California State University Northridge, Seattle Central Community College, St. Paul Technical Vocational Institute, the University of Tennessee, Gallaudet College, and New York University). These six institutions were known as the National Interpreter Training Consortium (NITC). This was the first step taken which, it is hoped, will eventually end with ITP accreditation that will ensure a reasonable amount of quality control. (Vidrine, p.321)

The second step was the result of the Comprehensive Rehabilitation Services Amendment of 1978, or PL 95-602. Funds were appropriated to underwrite twelve ITP's, doubling the original NITC number. The additional funding, which has continued to the present, did much to professionalize the training of interpreters. (Vidrine, p.322)

The third step toward improving ITP's came about in 1979. The Council of Directors of federally funded post-secondary institutions for the deaf, the NITC, and RID sponsored the first national Conference of Interpreter Trainers (CIT). (Witter, p.5) In 1981, CIT became an official organization with an executive board, constitution and bylaws. (Vidrine, p.324)

The purpose of CIT is to promote quality interpreter training through the realization of the following goals:

1. To provide professional development opportunities for interpreter trainers.
2. To develop liaison with other disciplines and organizations that interact with the interpreting field.
3. To provide an organizational structure for interpreter trainers.
4. To provide a vehicle for information sharing. (Vidrine, p.324)

The fourth step brings RID and CIT together in a joint effort to accredit ITPs. "On July 28, 1989, the Department of Education awarded CIT $30,641 to carry out the first year of a proposed two-year grant. . . . The project is called 'Implementation of a National Endorsement System for Interpreter Preparation programs. . . . Beginning November 1, 1989, the CIT/RID Joint Committee on Program Endorsement will officially begin its work." ("FIPSE Grant Awarded," p.5)

The CIT/RID Ad Hoc Committee on Educational Standards recently produced its suggested criteria for rating ITPs. It was interesting to me to make some comparisons of their suggested curriculum with that which appears in Interpreting for Deaf People, the manual produced by the Maine Workshop in 1965.

As one would expect, the CIT/RID curriculum includes some items that could not have been in the Maine curriculum, such as "theories of interpretation and transliteration," "RID evaluation process," "ASL linguistics," and "history and issues in interpretation and transliteration." In 1965 the word "transliteration" was unknown, and consequently, there are no theories, issues, or history of it to study. The RID evaluation process did not begin until 1972, and because ASL was not yet accepted as a language, its linguistic structure had not been explored.

The concept of transliteration did exist, but it went by the name of translation. It was not until the mid-seventies that "transliteration" became part of our vocabulary. The act itself, moving from PSE to English and vice versa, was not only known and practiced by us, but also received more attention in the Maine curriculum than did the act of interpretation. The reason for this lay in the belief that most interpreters would be working in educational settings where English was of prime importance.

One gets the impression that PSE was taught and learned first, then the student moved on to ASL. The ASL is talked about, however, as if it were the language of poorly educated deaf people. One gets the further impression from the Maine curriculum that ASL was not stressed because the call for its interpretation would not be as great, and that only advanced superior interpreters would accept such calls. This idea of teaching PSE first is clearly in evidence in most sign language classes taught at that time: the first task was always to master fingerspelling.

Since we did not yet believe that ASL was a language, we taught PSE as "sign language." What today we call ASL was to us "idiomatic" sign language used by deaf people whose English was severely limited. They signed that way only because they could not sign PSE, not because it was their choice. We believed students learned PSE more easily than ASL, which they did. We also believed that ASL could not be taught, but was learned by osmosis as one associated more and more with those deaf people who used it.

There was one item in the Maine curriculum which is conspicuous by its absence in the CIT/RID curriculum: practicum. It is difficult to see how an ITP can be complete without a practicum or internship for its students. As I said earlier, these CIT/RID suggested criteria are in draft form and the lack of practicum experience will probably be rectified in the final publication.

The training of interpreters has progressed considerably from the groping-in-the-dark stage to a level of sophistication which gives us assurance that we are on track. At least there are few people left who still contend that interpreters are born, not made. Yet there remains the nagging doubt that we still do not know enough about what qualities a person must have in order to be a successful interpreter. The research needed to tell us this is woefully lacking.

We need objective validation that what we believe about interpretation and the skills required to do it competently are accurate. We need knowledge underpinned with scientifically derived proof that our curricula contain the proper information and exercises that will develop interpretation competency. Until such data are available to us, we must be guided by whatever inner lights we have.

What little research has been done has been of a short-term nature, such as that done for doctoral dissertations; this research tends to raise more questions than provide answers. We need long-term, ongoing research that can follow interpreters over a period of years and find out what they are really made of. We need an interpreter research center to focus and manage long-term studies.

The great obstacle, of course, is money to underwrite a research center. Research on interpretation cannot compete with research in physical sciences, especially those that deal with life threatening diseases. In the social sciences most of the funding goes to research to alleviate the disorders of our society. Monies available for interpretation research must be judiciously spent, and long-term research seems to me the best investment.

One way to proceed would be for CIT and RID to approach a major university to apply for grants to support a research center. Neither professional organization, however, must participate actively in the conducting of the research, lest the results become tainted with bias. CIT and RID would stand ready as consultants when needed, and suggest areas where research is needed, but only the scientists should do the actual research. Furthermore, I believe those scientists ought not to come from the field of interpretation, ASL, or deaf education; we need fresh unprejudiced eyes to look at our problems, and see things oblivious to our eyes because we stand too near the problems.

The number of ITPs in this country has reached a critical mass, and this makes me feel that we are on the brink of some major, significant breakthroughs in the training of interpreters. Knowledge gained through the experience of all the trainers in the ITPs is accumulating rapidly and needs only to be systematized and disseminated. Knowledge in the form of curriculum materials seems to be the greatest lack in the ITPs. How wonderful it would be if there were an agency that would collect ideas, information, and experience from all the trainers of interpreters and transform them into books, audio tapes, and video tapes, and make them available to every ITP in the land.

The formation of CIT represented a giant step toward the professionalization of the field of interpretation. The goal voiced at the time RID was founded that put the training of interpreters at the top of our priorities is being realized. It has been a long, arduous climb and we have by no means arrived at the crest of the hill, but it is in view and there is no reason to fear that we will not attain it.

60

ETHICS

At one time or another we are all consumers of goods and services. Our decision to purchase an automobile, a television set, a can of soup, or to engage the services of an electrician are all influenced by our confidence in the name of the manufacturer or company. Our choice hinges upon the reputation of the manufacturer or company to turn out a product of expected quality, or perform a service that is dependable, and to stand behind the product or service. Cost is of lesser concern to us than confidence. We do not mind paying when we believe we are receiving quality for our money and can trust the producer to back up the product or service.

Name, reputation, expectations, dependability, quality, confidence, trust, these are the elements upon which the relationship between producer and consumer is based; they are the soil in which transactions, whether they involve goods purchased, services rendered, loans, or investments, are rooted. Without these essential ingredients, we operate on blind faith in the murky atmosphere of *caveat emptor*, and we are usually disappointed. These are also the essential ingredients of ethical behavior.

According to the *Oxford English Dictionary*, ethics is "the science of morals," "the moral principles or system of a particular leader or school of thought," "the moral principles by which a person is guided," "the rules of conduct recognized in certain associations or departments of human life." Webster's *New World Dictionary, Second College Edition*, says that ethics is "the study of standards of conduct and moral judgment; moral philosophy," "the system or code of morals of a particular person, religion, group, profession etc." An intelligent discussion of ethics requires that we accept the premise that ethics is based upon our concepts of right and wrong behavior, that is, morality.

Our society so frequently uses the word "moral" to refer to sexual behavior, that it is difficult for us to focus on the larger meaning of it. Webster's dictionary cited above defines "moral" as, "relating to, or dealing with, or capable of making the distinction between, right and wrong in conduct," "[pl.] principles, standards, or habits with respect to right or wrong in conduct." We cannot talk about ethics without agreeing that it relates to morality, but morality that deals with right and wrong behavior across the whole spectrum of human conduct, not just that narrow segment that deals with sexual conduct.

Furthermore, we must agree that right and wrong conduct is judged as such on the basis of its moral aspects. It is wrong, for example, to interpret against a background filled with a powerful light source, but let us concede that this is not a moral wrong. If we insist that all wrong behavior is, by definition, morally wrong, then we dilute the meaning of the word and make it devoid of efficacy. Intuition is our safest guide in determining whether wrong behavior is immoral or not.

A code of ethics could just as easily be called a code of morality, but that term carries the unfortunate connotation of acceptability or unacceptability in the realm of sexual behavior. Ethics does differ from morals in that it is the science, or study of morals. A code of ethics is a codification, or distillation, of rules that govern moral behavior. Professional codes of ethics are the rules of conduct by which the individual practitioner is expected to govern her/his conduct while performing the service of her/his profession. Codes of ethics do not address themselves to personal behavior outside the performance of professional services. An interpreter may act immorally as a private citizen, and still be a morally proper practitioner while rendering an interpretation, but if such information is known to the consumer, it will arouse suspicions as to the practitioner's trustworthiness. If, however, the immoral activity is illegal, then it becomes an issue to be addressed by our code of ethics, which unfortunately makes no mention of this eventuality.

Ethics deals with human character traits, an area where subjectivity is too prevalent for scientific analysis to operate effectively. We cannot turn to a body of empirical data, gathered from stringently controlled research, to help us decide what ought to go into a code of ethics. We are guided by an innate sense, accumulated over millennia of human history, of what is right and what is wrong. We have no alternative but to accede to Jimminy Cricket's dictum, "Always let your conscience be your guide." A code of ethics comes down to what we may call our collective professional conscience.

Another premise we must agree to, if intelligent discussion of ethics is to proceed, is that competency is not a matter of ethical behavior. Incompetency has to do with lack of skill that implies no immoral behavior. Competency has to do with skill, not ethics, and we will only confuse our thinking if we do not make this distinction. An interpreter renders a wrong interpretation because of lack of skill, or wears inappropriate clothing due to poor judgment, not because of a lack of moral sensibility.

Competency is a vital element upon which consumer trust and confidence are founded, but not the only one. Equally important is ethical behavior which has to do with character. The consumer's confidence in an interpreter rests on the dual foundations of competency and character. If either leg of this undergirding is weak or underdeveloped, the whole structure is jeopardized. Unhappily, both legs are not built of the same material, nor do they require the same length of time to develop.

The building blocks of competency are such things as intelligence, knowledge, training, experience, and talent. Some of the ingredients are innate, brought to us by the student who aspires to become an interpreter. Intelligence and talent, for instance, are not things a training program can instill; we work with whatever the student has. Our interpreter training programs provide the information for intelligence to convert into knowledge, and the opportunities for talent to develop into skills. Information and opportunity are the mortar that hold the blocks fast to one another.

Character is made of entirely different stuff. Hesitantly, we can list some of the building blocks of character, but we are dealing here with such intangible material that we cannot have the assurance we would like that all the essentials are accounted for. It is as difficult to pin them down as it is to prove in self-defense that one is a humble person. We can list good character traits, but we are hard put to say how they are realized.

Most of us would agree that a person of good character knows right from wrong, truth from falsehood; is honest, truthful, honorable, reliable, loyal, respectful, dependable; accepts responsibility for her/his decisions; exhibits taste, discretion, tact; and exercises good judgment. These modifiers, however, leave great latitude for definition, so we must again rely upon intuition for meaning. Granting agreement on definition, the big question is, how does a person develop good character?

We may suggest that certain circumstances during childhood contribute to the development of good character, such as a stable family background, economic security, good schooling, and good adult role models. Yet, how do we account for those people from broken homes, poverty, poor schooling, and environments devoid of adults to set good examples, who defy all the odds and grow up into sterling characters? We can only explain it by saying it is the work of intangible, unknown subtle forces of human nature.

One thing we can say with certainty is that ITP's have little effect on the development of character. Character is well constructed long before the student comes to us, and we can but point out flaws, cracks, and deficiencies in its construction. Only the student can make whatever repairs are required. Sadly, we cannot inculcate nor instill good character traits in those students who are lacking a full complement of them. We cannot measure the traits of good character, even if we could agree on what they are. It is cause for trepidation to realize that consumers' trust rests heavily upon something over which we have virtually no control.

Our code of ethics attempts to exercise control over specified behaviors, but it is merely an alarm system to warn us of behavior that will not be tolerated. No code of ethics can make any warranty as to the character of the practitioner. We may rightly be held responsible by the consumer for basic competency, but we cannot be held accountable for good character.

A code of ethics, to be effective, must deal only with ethical behavior, i.e. that behavior which springs from character, and must state its rules in terms that are as unambiguous as possible. It must distinguish between competent, professional behavior, and ethical, moral behavior. A set of guidelines takes care of the former, while a code of ethics addresses itself to the latter. Professional behavior is that which facilitates smooth, clear, and easy communication, elicits respect from consumers and colleagues, and exhibits commitment to our profession. Ethical behavior is that which obeys the rules of conduct in our code, thus eliciting trust from the consumer that we will always act morally in all our dealings with them.

Regrettably, our code of ethics commingles professional and ethical behavior, thus producing an imprecise compass to point out the correct direction for us to follow. Let us look at each article of the code and discuss whether it is an appropriate guideline for ethical or professional behavior.

ARTICLE I

"Interpreter/transliterator shall keep all assignment-related information strictly confidential."

This article clearly deals with ethical behavior. Discussion of its intent, however, is needed. A concession to confidentiality is made in the guidelines (Appendix D) with respect to sharing information with new trainees as long as precautions are taken to safeguard consumer anonymity. Additional concessions are needed.

With the increasing number of interpreters working in elementary and secondary educational programs, this stricture is becoming more and more impossible to observe. It is only a matter of time until educational interpreters in these settings become part of the teaching team; indeed this has already happened in many places. As such, they will be expected to share information regarding the deaf pupil. It is, after all, in the best interests of the deaf pupil, and the information shared with other professionals will be treated with confidentiality. It may be we will need a whole, separate code of ethics for these interpreters. This whole problem is dealt with in more detail in the section on Specialization on p.77.

Another concession that needs to be made is one that will help the interpreter to improve her/his skill. If, for example, an interpreter has rendered a message under difficult circumstances to a consumer with minimal language skills, and is uncertain that she/he did it as well as it could have been done, the interpreter ought to be able to check it out with a mentor, or colleague. If we are never allowed to do this, how can we check the validity of our work? The code of ethics ought to permit this kind of sharing while placing the burden of confidentiality on the interpreter/s with whom the information is shared.

There is another aspect of this article about which we must be aware. The court does not grant privileged status to interpreters. The only circumstance in which an interpreter may legally claim privilege is when she/he interpreted in the presence of one who does have privileged status, such as a lawyer, physician, psychiatrist, etc. Even if the situation involves interpreting for a lawyer and deaf client, only that information that passed between lawyer and client is privileged. Should the lawyer leave the room, and the consumer pass any information to the interpreter, that information is not privileged.

Our code of ethics makes no provisions for interpreters to reveal unprivileged information when ordered to do so by a court of law. As the matter now stands, interpreters must disobey a court order in order to to conform to the code of ethics. Until such time that privileged status is granted to interpreters, our code of ethics ought not to force interpreters to risk contempt of court proceedings against them. RID ought to work with other organizations of interpreters to legislate privileged status for interpreters of all languages in all interpreting situations.

ARTICLE II

"Interpreters/transliterators shall render the message faithfully, always conveying the content and spirit of the speaker, using language most readily understood by the person(s) whom they serve."

Although the intent of this article is focused on ethical behavior, the wording and the guidelines make it seem to be concerned with professional competency. The act of interpretation is to "render the message faithfully, . . . conveying the content and spirit of the speaker." If the interpreter cannot do this, then the interpreter is not competent. If, on the other hand, the interpreter intentionally distorts the message, or the spirit of the speaker, then the interpreter is unethical.

It is no easy task to ascertain a person's motive or intent, yet this element is vital in an attempt to differentiate between competent and ethical behavior. The best we can do is to warn the interpreter, and this can easily be accomplished by inserting the word, "intent," or some variation of it, in a rewording of the article.

ARTICLE III

"Interpreters/transliterators shall not counsel, advise, or interject personal opinions."

This article does not distinguish between behavior which results in counsel as to a disposition or decision, and that which results in clarification of meaning. If, for example, the deaf or hearing consumer asks the interpreter, "What do you think I should do?", there can be only one response and that is to decline an opinion for ethical purposes. But, if a misunderstanding, or non-comprehension of the message occurs, and the interpreter is aware of it, then the interpreter must interject. Indeed, it might even be considered unethical for the interpreter to remain silent.

Let us suppose an attorney, in the privacy of an office, is attempting to explain a complex aspect of law to the deaf consumer. The attorney uses the language attorneys are wont to use, the interpreter understands and renders the message in the appropriate register, but the deaf person does not understand. After several unsuccessful attempts, the interpreter asks permission from both consumers to suggest a different way to explain the law. Permission is granted, the explanation is made, and the deaf person understands. Neither the attorney nor the deaf person is likely to support anyone's allegation that the interpreter acted unethically.

Taking the above example one step further, suppose the deaf consumer still does not understand. The interpreter asks for permission to explain, permission is granted, the deaf person understands, then the interpreter tells the attorney exactly what she/he said in order to get confirmation that the explanation was correct. It may not be the responsibility of the interpreter to insure that the deaf person understands, but is it a violation of ethics to attempt clarification when the interpreter is aware of the problem and can clarify the message?

If the intention of the interpreter is to facilitate communication by clarifying difficult language, then the interpreter is acting in good faith. If the intention of the interpreter is to influence a consumer towards a particular point of view, then the interpreter is being unethical; the former has to do with competency, the latter with ethics. Article III ought to distinguish the two, proscribing one but not the other.

ARTICLE IV

"Interpreters/transliterators shall accept assignments using discretion with regard to skill, setting, and the consumers involved."

When an interpreter is asked to take an assignment, there is not always enough information available for the interpreter to make a judgment as to whether she/he is competent to carry out the assignment. If we refuse all assignments unless we are sure beyond a shadow of a doubt that we can do it, I fear many requests for interpreters will go uncovered. Usually the discovery that an interpreter is in over her/his head comes after the interpreter is on the job. That is when the decision is made whether to step aside or continue. It is clear that these determinations are matters of competency, in particular, the ability of the interpreter to assess a situation and her/his skills with regard to it. It is only a borderline ethical consideration.

Paragraph three of the guidelines (Appendix D) warns of situations where there is danger of the interpreter becoming emotionally involved with a consumer and thus unable to render an objective, unbiased interpretation. To move this article from a borderline ethical area into obvious ethical territory, the focus should be placed on the necessity to avoid conflicts of interest. An emotional, subjective involvement with a consumer is one kind of conflict of interest. Another, and perhaps more serious, conflict of interest involves a situation in which an interpreter has a stake, or vested interest in the outcome. It is unethical for interpreters not to disqualify themselves when they find themselves in such proceedings.

The ethical considerations under this article should extend to situations in which an interpreter might come into information that she/he can use later for personal gain or profit. We are probably talking about very rare occurrences, but we should try to touch all bases in our code.

ARTICLE V

"Interpreters/transliterators shall request compensation for services in a professional and judicious manner."

The only ethical consideration in this article has to do with a possible interpretation of, ". . .in a professional and judicious manner." It would be ethically unacceptable for an interpreter to threaten to inflict physical, emotional, mental, or economic harm upon a consumer who refused to pay the interpreter's fee. Granted, this is a bizarre reading of the clause, but it is a stretch of the imagination to claim that this article deals with ethical behavior.

Article V has to do with a business arrangement, a contractual agreement, whether written or not. How much an interpreter charges is not a matter of ethics, but business. The marketplace determines if the fee is reasonable. The consumer, usually the hearing one, who pays must decide if it is justifiable or exorbitant. An interpreter who charges too high a fee will soon be wanting for requests for her/his services. An interpreter who charges too little, or works *pro bono* will also likely go out of business, unless she/he has an independent source of income and interprets simply for the joy. In neither of these cases can the interpreter be accused of unethical behavior.

Interpreters who are much in demand ought to be compensated appropriately. If this arouses envy in their colleagues, the fault lies not with the interpreter, but rather with the colleagues. If we feel that an interpreter is gouging consumers, and bring the interpreter before the grievance committee on a charge that will be nearly impossible to sustain, we should rather ask why consumers use this interpreter. The search for the answers to this question will produce more fruitful results than trying to draw the line between "expensive" and "gouging." Whatever our orientation toward deaf people may be, we must accept the fact that many interpreters are in business to make the best living they can, and in the best tradition of the American entrepreneurial spirit, must be free to charge what the market will allow.

ARTICLE VI

"Interpreters/transliterators shall function in a manner appropriate to the situation."

The guidelines define "appropriate manner" to mean that the interpreter should be conscious of attire that might be distracting, and should conduct "oneself in all phases of an assignment in a manner befitting a professional." (Appendix D, Article VI, Guidelines, G) Further definition of what the befitting manner consists of is not given. Clothing and accessory habiliment can be distracting and even annoying to a deaf consumer, because they do tend to make it difficult for the eyes to screen them out in order to concentrate on the signing. As important as they are, they are not matters for ethical consideration.

To charge a female interpreter who perpetually wears clothing made of loud, clashing colors, or earrings that dangle wildly, or has inch long fingernails painted with green Day-Glo polish, with unethical behavior borders on the ludicrous. Equally ridiculous would be charges lodged against a male interpreter for wearing a beard, or a mustache which obscures the mouth. These may not be "conduct befitting a professional," and they certainly do call into question the judgment of the interpreter, but they are not cause to ring the ethical alarm bell.

Such inappropriate attire as described above could conceivably become an ethical issue if the intent of the interpreter was to disrupt proceedings. In such an event, we would be forced to conclude that the interpreter has other major problems that need attention. If the clothing of an interpreter is deemed to be indecent, it is a legal matter, not an ethical issue. Article VI stands in serious need of an overhaul.

ARTICLE VII
"Interpreters/transliterators shall strive to further knowledge and skills through participation in workshops, professional meetings, interaction with professional colleagues and reading of current literature in the field."

This is simply good advice, but not a rule for ethical behavior. Do we seriously believe interpreters will ever be charged, let alone convicted, of unethical behavior because they do not attend workshops, professional meetings, interact with colleagues, or read the literature? It is legitimate to question their commitment to professionalism if they do not engage in these activities, but we cannot question their ethics on these grounds.

ARTICLE VIII

"Interpreters/transliterators, by virtue of membership in or certification by the R.I.D., Inc. shall strive to maintain high professional standards in compliance with the code of ethics."

This article simply exhorts us to be professionals and to abide by the code of ethics.

To recapitulate, we need two statements: a code of professional conduct, and a code of ethics. The former could be called, Code of Professional Conduct, or Standards of Professional Behavior, or any such name that will outline what behaviors we expect from a professional interpreter. The behaviors to focus on are those that have to do with competency, skill, judgment, and common sense as to what is the right thing to do in a given situation. The following list might do as a starting point. Each item needs to be spelled out in detail, and illustrated with examples.

1. A professional interpreter is expected to participate in as many professional activities as possible, such as, local affiliate activities, workshops, conferences, and seminars.

2. A professional interpreter is expected to be well read, not only to keep abreast of developments in the field of interpretation, but also in current events, general knowledge, and fields of specialized work.

3. A professional interpreter is expected to encourage and support research in interpretation, and participate in it when asked.

4. A professional interpreter is expected to be able to assess the communication skills required for an assignment, and determine if she/he can meet the needs.

5. A professional interpreter is expected to know how and when to interrupt proceedings in order to clarify communication.

6. A professional interpreter is expected to know how to follow good business practice in setting and collecting fees.

7. A professional interpreter is expected to know how to dress appropriately in order not to impede communication.

8. A professional interpreter is expected to know under what conditions she/he may share interpretation experiences with other interpreters.

9. A professional interpreter is expected to be able to recognize situations that contain, or may contain, conflicts of interest, and know how to handle them.

Most, if not all, of these behaviors are contained in such books as those by Neumann Solow and Frishberg and are covered in ITP curricula, but they need to be distilled into a manual for each interpreter to have.

signed *may not be*

Toward a New Code of Ethics

Rather than merely rewrite the articles of our code, perhaps we should consider a different approach to the matter. We need to personalize our ethical standards, that is, to require each individual to make a commitment to uphold and abide by the code. This can be accomplished simply by requiring their notarized signature to the code. Not only will this bring home to each of us the gravity of the code, but it will also provide proof that we have read it, and agreed to abide by it.

It may be that an interpreter's oath would be more meaningful and carry more weight since it requires a personal pledge to fulfill the ethical requirements of our profession. With that in mind, the following code, presented in the form of an oath, could be the starting point for the development of a new set of rules for ethical behavior.

THE INTERPRETER'S OATH — *Lou's idea*

I solemnly swear that:

I will always interpret from American Sign Language to English, and from English to American Sign Language faithfully, truthfully, and accurately to the best of my ability in all situations in which I have agreed to interpret.

I will maintain confidentiality of all names, places, occasions and information to which I have been made privy as a result of my interpretations. If, in the best interests of a consumer, it is necessary to break confidentiality, I will do so in strict accordance with the procedures set forth in the RID Manual of Professional Standards.

I will accept no assignments or participate as an interpreter in no proceedings in which there may exist a conflict of interest for me, as defined in the RID Manual of Professional Standards.

I will use no information acquired during the course of my interpretations for my own or for others' personal gain or profit.

I will not become personally involved with the consumers of my interpretations in any manner that might compromise my objectivity, credibility, or integrity.

If I am found to be in violation of any part of this oath, or if I am ever convicted of a felony, I understand that I will forfeit my membership in, and my certification by the Registry of Interpreters for the Deaf, Inc.

Having been certified and having the information and guidelines of a manual of professional standards and a code of ethics, we lack only commitment in order to function as true professionals. As individual

persons, we are committed to the improvement of all mankind; as interpreters we are committed to providing the best service possible to deaf and hearing consumers; as professionals we are committed to upholding the standards of our profession, and its code of ethics.

LOOSE ENDS

Deaf Culture

Over the past decade there has been an increasing amount of discussion of deaf culture. I have wondered if "culture" is the proper term to use to describe this phenomenon, but I have no anthropological training to question its usage, so I leave that to those with the proper credentials. I fervently hope this is not another case of an appropriation of a well-defined term for our own purposes. That there is a separation between hearing and deaf people, there are not doubts, but I prefer to distinguish the two groups as "communities" until it is more convincingly demonstrated that there is in reality a deaf culture. In order to avoid confusion in this section, however, I will go along with the trend and use the label, "culture."

Before continuing this discussion of deaf culture, I pause to mention a new concept that has only recently been introduced into the field: third culture. Third culture has been defined as, "the community of Deaf and Hearing people who are involved in some way with each other." (Sherwood, p.6) It is further described as:

"Third culture is neither permanent nor stable. It varies constantly, depending on the immediate reason for the contact. It is a very flexible, changeable, and temporary phenomenon." (Bienvenu, p.1)

And:

"...third culture is a temporary phenomenon and that there are no frozen, established values and rules." (Bienvenu, p.5)

Third culture is an entity that exists only when there is interaction between deaf and hearing people; it is a temporal, transitory phenomenon. The important thing to bear in mind is "that it is ours;

that is, it belongs to both interpreters and to deaf people."
(Bienvenu, p.1)

The importance of third culture for us is that the act of interpretation takes place in it. Sherwood calls interpretation, "cross-cultural mediation."

> "Cross-cultural mediation is a communication process that occurs when a message between two or more principals who hail from distinct cultures is mediated by a third interpreter. The interpreter intercepts the message issued by the sender and decodes it, applies linguistic and cultural information appropriate to the target culture, encodes the transmitted material into a new form and sends the "new" message to the receiving principal. During this process, there is little or no interaction between the communication principals, except for any non-verbal communication that is available visually." (Sherwood, p.18)

This description of the process of interpretation shows a significant shift in orientation from the view held by interpreters during the early years of RID. Then, the process was viewed simply as translating a message from one language to another. We were not oblivious to cultural differences, we just did not think of them in those terms. Deaf people were different and we took those differences into account, but we thought of them primarily as linguistic differences. Deaf people, by and large, were not fluent in English, therefore, it was our task to act much like an electrical transformer and reduce the voltage of the incoming message to a more readily acceptable outgoing voltage.

Most of us had been raised in close contact with deaf people, so we were thoroughly familiar with deaf culture. We acted unconsciously in making whatever cultural adaptations were necessary to clarify the message. So ingrained were the cultural parameters that we never gave them much thought. Interpretation, in most cases, was the task of simplifying the English message.

We were skilled interpreters, without fully understanding the reasons for our success. We had internalized the culture of deaf people, and it stood us in good stead without our fully appreciating it. In the manual, *Interpreting for Deaf People* (Quigley), little attention was given to deaf culture in the proposed training of interpreters. The manual did stress the importance of getting to know deaf people, but the overwhelming emphasis was upon how to make the English clear in sign language.

It has taken us a few years to realize that fluency in ASL is not sufficient for success in the field of interpretation. As the source for interpreters who had grown up with intimate knowledge of the deaf culture began to dry up, interpreters were recruited and trained who had limited, if any, exposure to this information. Their preparation lacked this valuable input, and they were sent out to work not fully equipped to do the job. This, probably more than any other single factor, might account for the alleged widespread discontent with interpreters we are hearing about today. They are attempting to be cross-cultural mediators without sufficient knowledge of and experience with deaf culture, and an inadequate understanding and appreciation of the hearing culture. They are linguistically well trained, but culturally unprepared.

We may hope that the shift from the physically disabled perception of deaf people, to the sociolinguistic view will bring about more concentrated efforts to expose the student interpreter to deaf culture. In order for ITP's to do a better job of inculcating deaf culture in their curricula, however, much more research needs to be done. We need scientific evidence to establish just what deaf culture consists of. We have gone long enough on opinions; it is now urgent that we have documented verification, else we will once again find it necessary to back-up, revise, redefine, and rectify information.

After research has been done, the facts sifted and collated into well designed courses, and techniques for imparting the information refined, there will remain one more crucial step to take in the process of familiarizing ITP students with deaf culture: first hand experience of the culture. Knowledge alone will not suffice to prepare the student; what is called for is a way to expand the consciousness. The student must be placed in personal contact with deaf culture for an extended length of time in order to gain a full appreciation of its impact on the lives of deaf people.

If students of foreign languages aspire to become teachers or interpreters of that language, they know that sooner or later they must spend time living in the culture of the people who speak that language. It is absolutely necessary to be exposed on a daily basis to that culture in order to absorb it. Students thereby learn to put aside their cultural biases, and view the world through the eyes of a different cultural perspective. The exposure enlarges their consciousness, sharpens their sensitivity, reshapes their values, and in general makes them better human beings, as well as better teachers and interpreters.

Few of us would dispute the need for students in our ITP's to experience total immersion in the deaf culture; the problem is how this can be done. We cannot send students to a land of deaf people, nor even to a village, so where do they go? Deaf culture, unlike the other cultures of the world, does not exist within geographical boundaries. With few exceptions, deaf culture exists as a minority culture within a dominant culture. Thus total immersion can never be realized because deaf culture is in constant contact with hearing culture. The best approximation we can reach is within the context of a deaf family.

Those of us with deaf parents appreciate how much the experience of growing up in a deaf home contributed to our interpreting skills. There is no way to duplicate that experience for ITP students, but it can be approached. Much effort is expended on making opportunities accessible for people who for one reason or another are at a disadvantage, so let us now put forth effort to make the opportunity for experience of deaf culture accessible to ITP students. The effort will meet resistance, because the deaf culture has suffered numerous injustices from hearing culture and has substantial grounds for suspecting its motives. Still, we must strive to overcome objections in our attempts to train students more effectively.

Opposition to the placement of ITP students with deaf families can best be overcome by stressing the need for the deaf community to assume some responsibility for the training of interpreters. The deaf community must be convinced that it is a full partner in the venture of producing interpreters. Academic knowledge can go only so far in its preparation of interpreters, the deaf community must assist in supplying the vital ingredient of experience. If the deaf community refuses to participate in the training of interpreters, then it must share the blame for interpreters who are inadequately trained. The deaf community cannot protest, on the one hand, that too many interpreters have a poor attitude, are difficult to understand, are cold, aloof, and callous toward the deaf consumer, while on the other hand refusing to take part in the training of those interpreters.

Ideally, ITP students would live with deaf families during the period of their training. They would participate as full-fledged members in the lives of the families. ITP's would provide support services to the families in the way of financial subsidies for expenses incurred, counseling to resolve problems that arise, and interpretation free of charge. At the least, deaf families could adopt students and invite them into their homes from time to time, and take them to special events for deaf people.

Whatever arrangement can be arrived at, the preparation of interpreters will have taken a prodigious step forward by involving more deaf people. Indeed, we can make little further progress without the participation of the deaf community as a partner in the venture. Not only will the deaf community be an ally in producing the kind of interpreters it wants, but also it will be increasing the awareness of the general public as to its needs. When this happens, we can expect to see more interpreters become cross-cultural mediators worthy of the title.

Specialization

It is the nature of professions to begin as assemblies of generalists which evolve into sub-sets of specialists. General practitioners in the medical profession become cardiologists, otologists, ophthalmologists, and a wide array of specialists. Attorneys confine their practice to particular areas such as criminal law, contract law, business law, divorce, etc. Interpretation has followed this same path of natural evolution.

During the early years of RID, certificates of specialization were offered in legal interpreting and oral interpreting. At present, the specialist certificates are no longer granted, but will be re-instituted. In order to establish a specialist certificate, members must petition the National Certification Board (NCB) of RID. Petitions are judged on the basis of two criteria: (1) "Sufficient availability of training in the skills required for the requested certificate," and, (2) "Sufficient number of potential applicants to defray the costs of evaluation." (Cokely, 1986)

If, as I believe is the case, states will assume more responsibility for generalist certification, perhaps they should do the same for specializations. If it is indeed desirable for RID to turn over general certification to an organization or private company whose business is developing, administering, and scoring tests for professional organizations, then it would become this organization's task to attend to specialist certificates as well.

Putting aside the question of who should be responsible for specialist certification, let us explore the trend itself and what it means for the future of interpreters. Federlin took note of the increasing number of interpreters who do more than render interpretations. (Federlin) He spoke of interpreter-tutors, interpreter-evaluators (for vocational rehabilitation agencies), and interpreter-secretaries, and the need to revise ITP's to prepare interpreters for these kinds of work, and to revise the code of ethics to accommodate the settings in which these specialists work.

Since Federlin's article, there has been a tremendous growth of interpreters who work in educational settings with a concomitant increase in confusion as to what their roles are, how well prepared they are to meet the demands of the work, and the relevance of the code of ethics to their circumstances. A National Task Force on Educational Interpreting met in Washington, D.C. in March 1988 to address these and other issues. At this writing, a report of the deliberations and recommendations of the Task Force has not been published. It is encouraging to see that this area of specialization is getting the attention it deserves and that RID is one of the seven sponsoring organizations involved in the undertaking. (This should be a model for any specialist certification, in that RID should not attempt it on its own.)

It is fair to question, however, whether the situation in educational interpreting, which presently provides more opportunities for employment than there are interpreters, will endure for many more years. There is a growing reaction against mainstreaming in elementary and secondary educational settings, which might culminate in a swing of the pendulum back towards traditional settings. If such does occur, it will severely curtail the need for interpreters in mainstream programs.

There are probably corresponding growths in other specialities such as legal and medical interpreting, but there are no data to substantiate them. If these trends do exist and continue to expand, they may profoundly alter the character of RID in the coming years.

Demographic data for RID members do not exist, so any statement regarding the number of interpreters who work in various settings for specified lengths of time are assumptions and guesstimates at best. It is lamentable that we have not collected demographic data from our membership so that we might better meet our needs by knowing just who we are and what we are doing. We are lacking such basic information about our members as age, background, settings in which they work, and income. It would seem that a simple questionnaire sent to each member, and updated every few years, would provide us with the needed data. No profession can move intelligently without these basic statistics; rational decisions on policy are impossible without them.

In addition to demographic data, it would seem extremely useful to know such things as how large a population of deaf people is required to support one free lance interpreter? Where are the best job markets? This information would be helpful to interpreters when they are considering a move.

In addition to interpreters who work full time in educational settings, there are many interpreters, especially in large metropolitan areas, who work full time, or nearly so, in legal and medical settings. In order for them to fulfill their responsibilities, they often render ancillary services. Since they refer to themselves as interpreter-tutor, interpreter-aide, interpreter-office worker, etc., they have come to be known as hyphenates.

Ingram took issue with Federlin by describing the hyphenated interpreters as bilingual paraprofessionals rather than interpreters. (Ingram, p.6) His point is that there is a need for personnel who are fluent in ASL and English, and that attention needs to be focused upon producing them, but that they are not, strictly speaking, interpreters. His contention raises questions that could generate as much heated debate as did the oral interpreter controversy: Should an interpreter function as a paraprofessional? Is an interpreter specialist really a paraprofessional or a bilingual practitioner? Webster's *New World Dictionary, Second College Edition*, defines a paraprofessional as "a worker trained to perform certain functions. . . , but not licensed to practice as a professional." Federlin seems to say that a professional interpreter can also be a paraprofessional in a field other than interpretation. Ingram, on the other hand, seems to say that a professional interpreter ceases to be a professional in that field if she/he becomes a paraprofessional in another field.

The trend toward interpreters working in settings where they are called upon to render such services as filling out forms, explaining procedures, consulting with other professionals regarding dispositions of consumers, first-aid, counseling, clerical work, and teacher-aid work will continue and expand, and require RID to choose one of three options. RID may elect, (1) to continue as it is with the goal of providing services only to interpreters; (2) include interpreters who also work as paraprofessionals; (3) service interpreters, interpreter-paraprofessionals, and paraprofessionals who are not certified professional interpreters, but who do render interpretations.

RID has already made the decision by having a special interest group (SIG) of educational interpreters. This is, however, a *de facto* situation that has resulted because we have not yet defined the implications of the trend toward specialization. Federlin and Ingram began the process, but we have not followed through with it to a conclusion that will produce a *de jure* situation. If we leave it to happenstance, we will indeed enmesh ourselves in another fruitless controversy about who we are, and what we should be.

Our statement of philosophy must include our beliefs on this subject, and give us guidance to cope with this and other new trends and unforeseen circumstances of the future. Only if we are of one mind as to our position on the issue of interpreter-specialist-paraprofessional will we avoid an unwanted imbroglio of self-identity. We cannot make a clear-cut choice among the three options listed above until we are first clear about what we believe. We have made a choice, to be sure, by allowing the educational interpreters SIG, but it was a choice by default, not with purpose. Before other SIG's are formed we had best come to a resolution of our purpose for existence.

If, guided by our yet unwritten philosophy, we choose the first alternative, what might the outcome be? It would likely be that RID would become an organization of strictly free lance interpreters, since they are the only ones who function as generalists. A closer examination of this situation gives cause for some anxiety.

A large number of our profession who are not free lance interpreters, aspire to achieve that status, because it is seen as the most desirable. The attraction of choosing which jobs one will accept, setting one's own fee, and being responsible only to one's own authority are powerful. The image we have of the free lancer, however, may be a highly romanticized one. There are some, to be sure, who make an adequate living without pushing themselves to the brink of utter physical and mental exhaustion, but for too many the image is tarnished by the realities illustrated by Pamela Nygren's plight.

Over a seven month period, Nygren kept a detailed account of her work as a free lance interpreter in the Minneapolis area. Her total earnings for that period, after taxes and expenses came to $7,951.00, an average of $3.42 an hour (Nygren, p.71) (The editor noted that last year, Nygren earned about twice the generally accepted average for free lance interpreters.) According to her description, Nygren expended a tremendous amount of energy and endured much inconvenience to earn barely more than a minimum wage. As a result, she is incapacitated by Overuse Syndrome for her chosen career.

If Nygren's case is typical, and it very well may be, it is going to make free lance work less attractive. How can we convince people to enter a profession in which the prospects of earning a living that will support a family are dubious at best? How can we recruit young people into a career that may suddenly end in a few short years because of Overuse Syndrome?* What are the lures we can use to entice young people to commit themselves to a profession where the prospects of upward mobility, both financial and professional, are meager? If free lance interpretation is the answer for some, it is not for everyone. The alternative is specialization and paraprofessionalization.

Thus it would seem a safe prediction that if RID narrows its base to an organization for free lance generalists only, its membership will shrink considerably. Its impact upon the quality of interpretation services on the overall picture will be limited.

If RID opts for the second alternative, to include interpreters who also work as paraprofessionals, it will be necessary to create, or cause to be created, certification procedures, and separate sets of professional standards for each specialty. A new code of ethics ought to be of such nature as to cover all specialties. If RID follows this path it will lead to legal, medical, mental health, vocational rehabilitation, and other SIG's. All the specialists — later to be called paraprofessionals — will be certified interpreters, holding both general certification (CSC, CI, CT) and specialty certification.

---

*"Simply put, Overuse Syndrome is a condition which develops when a group of muscles are repeatedly used without allowing adequate rest periods." (Sanderson)

The primary difference between the second and third alternatives, that which would include free lance generalists, specialists, and paraprofessionals who are not certified interpreters, is obviously the inclusion of people who have little or no training to be interpreters. Precedent for including non-interpreters in RID membership exists. Our bylaws specify membership categories for students, supporters, organizations, and institutions. Additional categories could be established for those who work as paraprofessionals, but are not trained interpreters. The rationale would be to place ourselves in a position to help paraprofessionals do the best job possible as interpreters in their fields.

RID could, for example, encourage paraprofessional training programs to offer courses in ASL for their students. RID would help the programs design the courses to meet the needs for their fields. After graduation from a program, RID would provide resources for paraprofessionals to upgrade their skills in communication and interpretation.

Where no paraprofessional training programs exist, RID could approach regular training programs, to arrange with agencies for on-the-job experiences for ITP students to prepare them for paraprofessional work. Vocational counselor training programs, business colleges, and schools for professional psychologists are examples of on-going training programs where students could take special courses while they are in an ITP. A vocational rehabilitation agency, a social security office, and a hospital are examples of places for ITP students to gain on-the-job experience for paraprofessional work.

The third alternative would greatly broaden the base of membership of RID and allow its commitment to professionalism to have its greatest impact. If it all sounds too idealistic, too grand, and unrealizable, let us remind ourselves of the Biblical warning that, "Where there is no vision, the people perish."

Although it is important that RID consider carefully which path it will follow, for the choice will alter its basic character, it is even more important that it make a definite choice. The matter is too urgent to be left to the whims of expediency. Changes in our society are occurring too rapidly to allow us merely to drift into one or another course of action. We must act with purpose, reason, and dedication, else forces over which we exert no control will guide and shape our destiny for us.

Local Affiliates

We have had meager success in finding ways for our membership to participate in the deliberations and decisions that have determined the nature and course of our organization. In the beginning there was no representation of the wishes of the membership; the board made all decisions.

In 1970 the first step was taken to solicit input from members when we held our first convention. Although members had a vehicle for expressing their views through discussion and debate at the conventions, it was not until 1985 that power to make final decisions was transferred from the board to the membership.

The opportunity for input, however, remains relatively limited. The main avenue for expressing opinions is the biennial conventions, yet less than twenty-five percent of the membership attends them. The ideas and views of an overwhelming majority are never heard unless they are reported through articles and letters in our official organ, *VIEWS*. A casual perusal of any issue of *VIEWS* will reveal that such reporting is minimal, and often comes from members who do attend conventions. We need to make ourselves more accessible to each other's views and become more responsive to our collective will. If the majority is to rule, we must find a way to discern more clearly what the majority wants.

We make motions that lead to resolutions which are then voted on at a convention, or are submitted to a referendum through *VIEWS* to be voted upon. The majority of votes cast, however, does not necessarily represent the will of the majority of the membership. If less than half the membership votes, how can we have any certainty as to what the majority feels? Everyone has an opinion, but far less than a majority bothers to make that opinion known by voting. It is mainly through discussion that opinions come to light. Unfortunately, much of the discussion occurs after the fact, and too often creates confusion rather than consensus. Dissent is welcome, but it ought to precede the fact and not follow in an aftermath of discontent, and it ought not to occur exclusively at conventions.

If conventions and published referenda are inadequate methods for measuring the pulse of our membership, then we are left with the conclusion that a different approach is needed. It would seem that whatever structure a new approach might take, the local affiliate must play a larger, more vital part in it. Instead of being mere dangling appendages to the national organization, local affiliates must become the foundation upon which the national organization rests. A democratic institution functions best when it is ruled by its grass roots, and the local affiliates represent the soil in which our roots are imbedded.

Local affiliates ought to be so constituted as to exert the major influence on how we govern ourselves. Local affiliates ought to be in close touch with local deaf communities in order to sense their feelings and be aware of changing circumstances that directly impact on the field of interpretation. Local affiliates must pursue more rigorously a public information program to enlighten consumers. Local affiliates must implement and administer a viable grievance procedure to insure fairness for consumers and interpreters. Local affiliates must, in concert with state

NAD associations, establish and maintain close contact with state legislatures and agencies that affect interpreting services. Local affiliates must sponsor workshops to upgrade interpreters' skills. Local affiliates must become an efficient conduit for channeling information upwards to the national organization, rather than the other way around, which seems to be their primary function at present.

Perhaps RID needs to adopt a pattern of representation similar to that of the United States Congress. Instead of regional representatives, there could be local affiliate representatives who are sent to conventions as agents to furnish the needed input of local members. Conventions would, in effect, become congresses, at which only representatives from local affiliates would vote. Under the present system, decisions made at conventions represent the wishes of those who can afford to be there. The majority of members cannot attend for financial reasons, or because they cannot take off from work. We have an inequitable situation in which those who do not attend conventions are, in effect, disenfranchised. It is not, however, so much the necessity to get everyone to vote, as it is to get everyone involved in a discussion of the issues before they vote.

Agendas for convention business could be developed from local affiliate discussions of issues they feel need to be addressed, and how they should be resolved. Mailing ballots to individual members has proven to be an ineffective technique to ascertain the feelings and beliefs of the members. Far less than half the ballots are returned, so a minority of members still make the decisions. A better way would be to instruct local affiliates to conduct referenda, thus making them the forums where the crucial activity of discussion takes place.

We need to give much more attention to developing the strength of local affiliates. Workshops need to be conducted to train local affiliate personnel in ways to operate efficiently within their communities and states, and within the national organization. There may even come a day when some local affiliates will have full time staff to conduct their business.

At the El Paso Convention, 1989, the issue of dual membership was resolved. The issue was that many local affiliates had large numbers of members who were not members of RID. The consequences of this state of affairs were that people who were not members of RID could make decisions which directly affect RID. In El Paso, the decision was made that members of local affiliates who wished to have voting privileges in that affiliate, must hold membership in both the affiliate and the national organization.

The extent of the problem was considerable, according to Witter-Merrithew, who said that the number of members of local affiliates who did not belong to RID was estimated to vary between 50 and 60 percent

(Witter-Merrithew). It was cause for trepidation to realize that the potential existed for a majority of non-RID members to control and direct the activities of a local affiliate.

On professional grounds there was no defensible rationale for allowing people to be voting members of a local affiliate, but not requiring them also to be members of RID. It was untenable to imagine we could move into the remaining decade of this century and into the twenty-first century with the extraneous weight of this burden taxing our resources.

In some locations, the affiliate functioned as a civic or social organization that conducted very little business *per se* (Ibid., p.3) People joined for all kinds of reasons, but obviously not for professional ones. The argument against dual membership usually rose from objections people had to the cost of RID dues.

"First, let's look at the affiliate chapter members who are currently not part of RID. A major reason these members give for not joining RID is one of cost. Since certified members must pay their dues in order to maintain their certification, the individuals who are not joining are not certified and would fall in the Associate membership category. Dues for an Associate member are now $44 per year, or $3.66 per month. This is less than the price of a Big Mac, Coke, and fries; less than the price of a movie; and certainly less than the price of a pair of jeans!" (Helander, p.4)

Surely people in quest of professionalism could have afforded the dues. The only explanation for their resistance to joining RID that makes sense to me is that they were not professionals. Whatever their reasons for wanting to be members of the affiliate were, there is truly only one valid reason and that is to grow professionally and contribute to the growth of the profession. If these people choose to withdraw their membership from local affiliates as a result of the El Paso decision, I should think we are the better for it. RID cannot afford, either financially or professionally, to support people who have no interest in advancing the profession.

Advocacy

In March 1988, a historic event took place on the campus of Gallaudet University. The students, reacting to the selection of a hearing person to be the new president of the university, revolted and succeeded in overturning the board of trustees' decision. For the first time, Gallaudet had a deaf president. The occasion evoked tumultuous jubilation in the deaf community throughout the land. Hearing people who had never heard of Gallaudet, spoke of the event as a landmark in human affairs. Never had deaf awareness among the general public been as pervasive as it was on this occasion. Yet, amidst the joyous celebration, a dark omen loomed.

Stories drifted about of interpreters who were subjected to verbal abuse because they interpreted for representatives of the board of trustees. The interpreters were perceived as supporting the board's selection of a hearing president, simply because they were carrying out their professional obligations as an interpreter. Even if the stories are not true, the mere fact that they were circulated should serve as a warning to us.

They warn us that we have delayed too long in developing an effective consumer education program. RID ought to create a short-term course to be taught in schools for deaf children, in post secondary educational settings for deaf adults, in adult education programs, and in any program for deaf people. The deaf consumer must be taught how best to utilize an interpreter, by knowing the roles and responsibilities of both consumer and interpreter. To postpone further the education of deaf consumers is to prolong misconceptions, frustration, and discontent.

The stories also warn us to remember that RID is not an agency for advocacy, except to advocate for interpreters. As individuals we do support the deaf community in its struggle to achieve its rights, to gain accessibility, and to put down discriminatory practices, but as interpreters we are neutral in the struggle. We cannot become involved in the campaign without jeopardizing our credibility as objective practitioners of our profession. In every aspect of the conflict between the deaf and hearing communities, both consumers must have interpretation, and unless we scrupulously preserve our neutrality, one side or the other will accuse us of supporting their adversary simply because we are interpreting for it.

In a court of law, if a deaf person has been accused of a heinous crime, the interpreter is never perceived as condoning the crime simply because she/he is interpreting for the defendant. That same attitude must be fostered towards interpreters when they work in controversial situations, such as the one that occurred at Gallaudet, especially when they become as intense and generate as much emotion as did that one. When the interpreters find themselves enmeshed in a stormy encounter between two parties, they must not be seen as advocates of either side merely because they are interpreting for one side or the other. The only way to prevent this misperception is to maintain a stringent neutrality on all issues.

This is hard advice to live with, especially when we are witnesses to the many injustices perpetrated upon deaf people. Our natural instincts for the just and equal treatment of all human beings is offended by the inequitable ways deaf people are dealt with. It requires diligent self-control to restrain our desire to speak out against prejudice and ignorance, yet we must exercise that discipline in order to preserve our objectivity, which is our only shield against becoming biased ourselves.

Even as private citizens we risk our credibility when we join in protests against unjust practices against deaf people. If we put ourselves among the ranks of a partisan movement, how can we expect to be seen as anything less than traitors to that movement if we accept an assignment to interpret for the opposition? People ought to be able to understand how we can put aside our own personal feelings and do our job, and that doing our job does not imply we have abandoned our beliefs, or that we are wishy-washy in our convictions. People being what they are, however, will too often misconstrue our intentions. Perhaps, with an effective consumer education program, and with time, we can help consumers appreciate our circumstances, and allow us to be both objective practitioners and advocates for what we believe.

In an open letter from the RID board, we came dangerously close to advocating a point of view that could undo all our efforts to claim objectivity for our work.

"As this issue goes to press, we wish to heartily congratulate the students of Gallaudet University, Washington, D.C. campus for their achievements during the week of March 6-13, 1988. Their protest and demonstrations were well organized, direct and yet peaceful, which enabled them to place their point-of-view in the public eye and in a positive and exemplary way. Their goals and demands were inspirations to millions of deaf and hearing-impaired persons in many nations and they deserve to be proud of what they have accomplished in the name of so many.

RID acknowledges the historic significance of the Gallaudet victories. . . advances that will have profound impact on the Deaf Community for years to come. And we are particularly pleased that individual RID members gave unstintingly of their time, effort and dedication. . . day and night. . . during that unforgettable week, in the cause of the Deaf Community's fight for increased self-determination.

We are sending congratulations to I. King Jordan on his appointment as Gallaudet University's President and Phil Bravin on his selection as chair of the Gallaudet Board of Trustees. RID looks forward to creative ways of collaborating with the new leadership at Gallaudet University." ("Open Letter from RID Board of Directors and National Office," p.1)

It is difficult to find fault with the board and national office staff for expressing sentiments which we all share. All of us as individuals surely rejoice at the outcome of the events at Gallaudet, yet is it wise to purse a congratulatory course which may impugn our ability to work objectively? We do, after all, serve hearing consumers as well as deaf consumers. What does an official statement such as this one say to the hearing community? Will it raise doubts in their minds as to our trustworthiness? The results of the Gallaudet student revolt are so patently right that even the hearing community overwhelmingly gave them its full support. Most likely little damage has been done to our credibility as neutral, objective practitioners. Let us beware, however, of setting a precedent that might endanger our professional integrity. Let us, instead, learn to walk the narrow path between advocacy as individuals, and objectivity as professional interpreters.

KNOTS

I have felt several emotions as I wrote this book: joy, dismay, excitement, anger, and hope, to mention the main ones. Joy because of how much we have accomplished; dismay at how much we have erred; excitement for the future; anger at our dilatoriness; and hope for our success. The one emotion I did not, nor do not feel, is despair.

Like Sisyphus, condemned for eternity to roll a great stone up a hill only to watch it roll down again, we have climbed some steep cliffs only to slide back somewhat. We have gone down some dead ends, and had to retrace our steps. We have made proclamations and performed acts that have come back to haunt us. Still in all, there has been considerable movement forward. I am filled with assurance that we will continue to move forward, and will commit fewer mistakes to deflect our progress.

My purpose in writing this book was not to find fault and blame for our mistakes, but rather to describe, in a manner as free of references to personalities as I could, how and where we have erred. We learn from our mistakes far more than we do from our successes, and it was with this thought that I dwelled more on what we did wrong, or did not do at all, rather than on what we did right. I believe it is necessary to see where we have been in order to understand where we are and to have a vision of where we want to go.

I hope I speak for all of those who have been involved with RID for all of its 25 years, when I say that I welcome enthusiastically the younger generation of members in whose hands our future rests. I have not the slightest doubt they will guide RID with sure and firm hands. I ask them to look at our past and learn and not to be despondent about our shortcomings, but rather to study them in order to avoid their like again.

I close with this anecdote which I hope will be of some value to you.

I began my career as an interpreter under conditions I can only characterize as a baptism of fire. The occasion was the meeting of the Southern Baptist Convention in Houston, Texas, sometime in the early fifties. I was around 19 or 20 years old and still a student at Baylor University.

The convention hall seemed to me to be large enough to seat 10,000 people, but I am sure my terrified eyes exaggerated the number; nevertheless, there was a great multitude. The deaf people were seated at the end of the balcony to the speaker's right in full view of all the crowd. It was a hot, muggy night, and there was no air conditioning.

Lillian Beard was the official interpreter; I was her back-up support. She had decided, however, that the time had arrived for me to get my feet wet, and anyone who knows Lillian will attest to the fact that her winsome way of convincing you to do something is irresistible. So, before the meeting got underway, she informed me that she would handle the preliminaries, and I would take the sermon.

I nodded feebly that I would do my best, and sat down to compose myself. I was wracked with dread that I was going to make a complete fool of myself, faint from mortification, and tumble out of the balcony onto the laps of the unsuspecting people below. I think it was the only time my knees shook while I was sitting. My hands trembled, my pulse rate shot up, and I began to hyperventilate.

Though the temperature was probably not more than eighty degrees, all the hot air in that hall seemed to have congregated at our end of the balcony and resisted all efforts to be moved by fans or open windows. The humidity must have been near a 100 percent to judge by the amount of perspiration that was accumulating around my collar. To make matters worse, I was wearing a grey, wool flannel suit, double-breasted, so it could not be unbuttoned without making me look more dishevelled than I felt I already looked. I was too overwhelmed with fear to think to ask if I could remove my coat, and any way, if the preacher was wearing his, I felt obliged to wear mine.

The preliminaries of announcements, songs, and prayers lasted about half an hour with Lillian handling them in the wonderfully inimitable style which made her the greatest interpreter I have ever seen. As the last prayer drew to a close, she smiled beatifically at me, nodded, then sat. Feeling as if I were climbing the steps of a gallows, I stood, pressed my back firmly against the balcony rail, and hoped it would hold me against the indignity of plunging 20 feet to a humiliating death. For a brief moment I wondered if I ought not to warn the people below of the danger they were in so they could all get up and move.

If you have ever had to follow a hard act, you have some appreciation of how I, a rank neophyte, felt having to follow Lillian Beard, my idol. I trusted the deaf folk to forgive me, so when the preacher began to speak, there was nothing for it but to begin to flap my arms. He went on speaking for forty-five minutes, then, as Baptists are wont to do, he held a forty-five minute invitation for all who wished to publicly testify as to their waywardness and rededicate their lives to come forward to the pulpit. I persevered through the entire hour and a half. My suit became a steam bath entrapping all my heat within it. It was so wet that I could wring moisture from it, even after I had gotten to Lillian's house that night.

During the last half-hour of the ordeal, I cast numerous furtive, pleading glances at Lillian in the hope she would declare that I had suffered enough and would put me out of my misery by relieving me. She returned my supplications with that memorable smile and a countenance that told me I was in it for the duration. Never have I felt such elation as I did when I heard that final, "Amen," and I collapsed into my seat.

Later that night, after I had hung my sopping wet suit to dry, Lillian, her dear husband, Louis, and I sat around the kitchen table munching on snacks while she critiqued my performance. I do not recall what she said, only that Louis kept chuckling between mouthfuls.

That is how we broke in new interpreters in the old days. Our motto was: "Throw it in the pond and see if it floats." We watched, then tried, then listened to the feedback. Deaf people got into it too with a generous amount of suggestions for betterment. I have often wondered how many interpreters we lost in that pond.

We have journeyed a long way from those hair-raising graduations from WADLU, but one thing remains as true today as it was back then: anxiety goes with the territory. I still get nervous before I interpret for a large crowd, and I hope I always will. The day I feel no tinge of fear is the day I quit interpreting. That little knot in my stomach reminds me that I do not know it all yet, I still make mistakes, there is still room to grow, I can still get better. When that knot is gone, I will plateau and cease to develop. So when that knot appears in your stomach, be grateful and remind yourself why it's there.

REFERENCES

A Workshop To Activate Interpreting Services for the Deaf, San Francisco, 1966, unpublished mimeograph of the proceedings.

Application for Research or Demonstration Grant, Department of Health Education, and Welfare, Vocational Rehabilitation Administration, Washington, D.C., "To Implement the Successful Professionalization of the Registry of Interpreters for the Deaf," July 1, 1967.

Bienvenu, M.J., "Third Culture: Working Together," *Journal of Interpretation,* Vol. IV, 1987, RID, Rockville, MD, p.1-12.

"Board of Directors Action (November 18-21, 1982)," *Views,* Vol. VIII, no. 3, 1983, p.3.

Cokely, Dennis, Letter to Diane Castle, November 25, 1986.

Cokely, Dennis, "When Is a Pidgin Not a Pidgin? An Alternate Analysis of the ASL-English Contact Situation," *Sign Language Studies,* Spring, 1983, Linstock Press, Silver Spring, MD, p.1-24.

Council on Education of the Deaf, *Interprenews,* Vol. V, no. 3, March, 1979, p.7.

Falberg, Roger M., *The Language of Silence*, Wichita Social Services for the Deaf, Wichita, KS, 1962.

Fall Board Meeting—Dallas, Texas, *Views,* Vol. III, no. 3, December 1980, p.4.

Federlin, Tom, "Sign Language Interpreters. . . The Changing Role," *Views,* Vol. VI, no. 1, October, 1979, p.4 (Reprinted from the November 1978, *Deaf American* by permission of the author).

"FIPSE Grant Awarded," *CIT News*, Vol. IX, no. 4, September 1989.

Fischer, Susan D., letter to the editor, *Views,* Vol. VI, no. 3, February 1980, p.4.

Frishberg, Nancy, *Interpreting: An Introduction,* RID, Silver Spring, MD, 1986.

Fritsch-Rudser, Steven, "Interpreting: Difficulties in Terminology," *The Interprenews,* Vol. V, no. 3, 1979, p.1.

Helander, Carol B., "Dual Membership: A Response," *Views,* May 1988, p.3-4.

Higgins, Dan D., *How to Talk to the Deaf,* J.S. Paluch Co., Inc., Chicago, IL, 1942.

Ingram, Robert M., "Focus," *Views,* Vol. VI, no. 1, October 1979, p.6.

Lane, Harlan, *When The Mind Hears:A History of the Deaf,* Random House, New York, 1984.

Long, J. Schuyler, *The Sign Language, A Manual of Signs*, Dorothy Long Thompson, Omaha, NE, 1944 (Reprint of second edition; original copyright dated 1918).

Lowell, Edgar, personal correspondence, August 26, 1988.

Michaels, J.W., *A Handbook of the Sign Language of the Deaf,* Home Mission Board Southern Baptist Convention, Atlanta, GA, 1923.

Neumann Solow, Sharon, *Sign Language Interpreting: A Basic Resource Book,* National Association of the Deaf, Silver Spring, MD, 1981.

Nygren, Pamela, "The Real Cost of Freelance Interpreting in the State of Minnesota," *Journal of Interpretation,* Vol. IV, 1987, RID, Rockville, MD, p.69-72.

"Open Letter from RID Board of Directors and National Office," *Views,* March 1988, p.1.

"Proposed Philosophy Statement of RID, Inc.," *Views,* January 1988, p.6.

Quigley, Stephen P., ed., *Interpreting for Deaf People,* U.S. Department of Health, Education, and Welfare, Vocational Rehabilitation Administration, Washington, DC, 1965.

"RID Board of Directors Meeting, (November 10-13, 1983)," *Views,* Vol. IX, no. 3, November/December 1983, p.7.

"RID Enters New Decade," *Views,* Vol. VI, no. 3, February 1980, p.1.

Report by the Ad Hoc Committee on Recertification and Maintenance, prepared for the 1989 RID Convention in El Paso, Texas.

Sanderson, Gary, "Overuse Syndrome Among Sign Language Interpreters," *Journal of Interpretation,* Vol. IV, 1987, Rockville, MD, p.74.

Sherwood, Bonnie, "Third Culture: Making It Work," *Journal of Interpretation,* Vol. IV, 1987, RID, Rockville, MD, p.13-24.

Smith, Jess M., ed., *Workshop on Interpreting for the Deaf,* proceedings published under VRA Grant No. 460-T-64, 1964.

Stokoe, William C., Jr., *Sign Language Structure: An Outline of the Visual Communication Systems of the American Deaf,* Studies in Linguistics, University of Buffalo, Buffalo, NY, 1960.

"Straw Vote on RID Philosophy Statement," *Views,* January 1988, p.6.

Taylor, Lucile Neesam, ed., *Proceedings of a Follow-Up Workshop on Interpreting for the Deaf* (mimeographed), Department of Health, Education, and Welfare, Washington, DC, 1965.

Vidrine, Jacqueline, "An Historical Overview of Interpreter-Training Programs," *Proceedings of the Fourth National Conference of Interpreter Trainers Convention*, RID Publications, 1984.

Witter, Anna and Carlson, Becky, "National Conference of Interpreter Trainers," *Views*, Vol. VI, no. 2, December 1979.

Witter-Merrithew, Anna, "President's Column," *Views,* May 1988, p.2-3.

Woodward, James, *How You Gonna Get to Heaven if You Can't Talk to Jesus, On Depathologizing Deafness,* T.J. Publishers, Silver Spring, MD, 1982.

APPENDIX A

Constitution of the Registry
of
Interpreters for the Deaf

ARTICLE I

Name

The name of this organization shall be the Registry of Interpreters for the Deaf (further known as RID).

ARTICLE II

Purposes

This organization is to be a non-profit organization of interpreters and translators for the deaf, the purposes of which shall be:

1. To prepare, maintain, and distribute a registry of accredited interpreters and translators.

2. To establish certification standards for qualified interpreters and translators.

3. To recruit qualified interpreters and translators, both manual and oral.

4. To work for the training and advancement of qualified interpreters and translators.

5. To prepare literature dealing with methodology and the problems of interpreting and translating.

6. To prepare a guideline of terminology applicable to the various aspects of interpreting and translating.

7. To work within the framework of organizations of the deaf insofar as possible.

8. To adopt and promote a code of ethics.

ARTICLE III

Membership

Section 1. Charter members. All persons present at the establishment of this organization at Ball State Teachers College, Muncie, Indiana, on June 16, 1964, who declared themselves as qualified interpreters and persons who secured membership as interpreters and translators through sponsorship of another charter member prior to January 1, 1965, shall be known as charter members.

Section 2. Sustaining members. All deaf persons, not declaring themselves as qualified interpreters, present at the organizational meeting, shall be known as sustaining members with sponsorship privileges. Upon the death, resignation, or change in status of membership of charter sustaining members, successors shall be chosen by the remaining sustaining members, subject to the approval of the executive board.

Section 3. Active members. After January 1, 1965, and until definite certification procedures go into effect, any person may become an active member through sponsorship by two other members of the RID.

ARTICLE IV

Officers

The officers of this organization shall be a president, vice president, secretary-treasurer, and two board members at large, one of whom shall be a sustaining member. Their terms of office shall be for four years.

ARTICLE V

Executive Board

Section 1. Composition. The executive board of this organization shall consist of the president, vice president, secretary-treasurer, board members at large, and members of the board of examiners.

Section 2. Authority. Authority shall be vested in the executive board to govern this organization, by directing its policies and operations in all matters relating to the purposes for which it was formed.

ARTICLE VI

Board of Examiners

Section 1. Composition. The executive board shall appoint two members of the board of examiners from each of the nine regions of the United States as specified by the bylaws.

Section 2. Function. The board of examiners shall serve as the accrediting body of the RID once definite procedures have been established. They shall also promote the work of the RID within their respective regions and exercise other functions delegated to them.

ARTICLE VII

Meetings

Section 1. Official call. Meetings of the RID shall be subject to the call of the president, with 25 members in good standing constituting a quorum.

Section 2. Frequency. At least one meeting shall be held every four years unless the executive board rules that such a meeting is not possible due to circumstances or inability to meet in accordance with provisions of the bylaws.

ARTICLE VIII

Dissolution

On the dissolution or winding up of this ____(Corp./Assoc.)____ its assets remaining after payment of, or provisions for payment of, all debts and liabilities of this ____(Corp./Assoc.)____ shall be distributed to a non-profit fund, foundation, association or corporation that is organized and operated exclusively for educational purposes which has established its tax-exempt status under Section 501(c) (3) of the Internal Revenue Code, as amended. If the ____(name of organization)____ meets the above requirements, this organization should be considered as primary beneficiary in final distribution of net assets.

Amendments

Section 1. Proposals. Amendments to the constitution may be proposed by the executive board or in writing and signed by ten or more members.

Section 2. Submission. Proposed amendments shall be submitted by either of the following methods: (a) At a called meeting of the RID with 25 members in good standing constituting a quorum and a two-thirds vote of those voting necessary for adoption; (b) by a mail vote with a minimum of two-thirds of the members in good standing voting within a 30-day period and a two-thirds vote necessary for adoption.

APPENDIX B

First Bylaws of the
Registry of Interpreters for the Deaf

ARTICLE I

Membership

Section 1. Charter members. Charter members of this organization are those members who were enrolled before the January 1, 1965, deadline as specified by the constitution.

Section 2. Sustaining members. Sustaining members of this organization are deaf persons who were enrolled as charter members at the organizational meeting on June 16, 1964, or those who are selected as their successors as provided by the constitution. Upon the death, resignation, or change in status of membership of a sustaining member, the secretary-treasurer shall poll the remaining sustaining members as to their preference for a successor. The preference, expressed by majority vote, shall be certified by the secretary-treasurer to the executive board for its approval. In event the nomination of a successor is not approved, the secretary-treasurer shall conduct a similar poll until a successor is approved.

Section 3. Active members. Active members shall be those sponsored by two other members of the RID after January 1, 1965, and until definite certification procedures go into effect. Persons wishing to enroll as active members shall complete an application form which shall be endorsed by two other members in good standing. This application fee, accompanied by the initiation fee, shall be sent to the secretary-treasurer for processing.

ARTICLE II

Dues

Section 1. Initiation fee. The initiation fee for all members shall be five dollars, payable at the time an application is submitted.

Section 2. Annual dues. Annual dues shall be two dollars, payable July 1 of each year, effective July 1, 1966. Good standing shall be contingent upon payment of annual dues before September 30 of each year.

Section 3. Assessments. Assessment may be levied on all members by action of the executive board. Such assessments shall not exceed three dollars during a fiscal year beginning July 1.

ARTICLE III

Officers

Section 1. President. The president of this organization shall preside over all called meetings as provided for in the constitution, and at meetings of the executive board. He shall preside over deliberations of the executive board or of the entire membership which may be conducted by mail. He shall appoint such committees as may be provided for in the bylaws and other committees he may deem necessary in promoting the purposes of the organization. He shall assign specific duties to the members of the executive board.

Section 2. Vice President. The vice president shall fill the office of the president when the president is, for any reason, unable to perform the duties of his office.

Section 3. Secretary-treasurer. The secretary-treasurer shall keep membership records, process applications for membership, act as custodian of the funds of this organization, and perform other duties as specified by the bylaws.

Section 4. Board members at large. Board members at large shall perform duties assigned them by the president.

Section 5. Members of the board of examiners. Members of the board of examiners shall assist the president and the secretary-treasurer in promoting the work of the RID within their respective regions. When certification procedures go into effect, it shall be the duty of the board of examiners to clear applications within their respective regions.

Section 6. Regions. Regions of this organization shall be:

Region I	Connecticut
	Maine
	Massachusetts
	New Hampshire
	Rhode Island
	Vermont
Region II	Delaware
	New Jersey
	New York
	Pennsylvania
Region III	District of Columbia
	Kentucky
	Maryland
	North Carolina
	Puerto Rico
	Virginia
	West Virginia
Region IV	Alabama
	Florida
	Georgia
	Mississippi
	South Carolina
Region V	Illinois
	Indiana
	Michigan
	Ohio
	Wisconsin

Region VI	Iowa
	Kansas
	Minnesota
	Missouri
	Nebraska
	North Dakota
	South Dakota
Region VII	Arkansas
	Louisiana
	New Mexico
	Oklahoma
	Texas
Region VIII	Colorado
	Idaho
	Montana
	Utah
	Wyoming
Region IX	Alaska
	Arizona
	California
	Hawaii
	Nevada
	Oregon
	Washington

ARTICLE IV

Executive Board

The executive board, consisting of the president, vice president, secretary-treasurer, board members at large, and the members of the board of examiners, shall govern this organization, by directing its policies and operations in all matters relating to the purposes for which it was formed.

ARTICLE V

Resignations

Section 1. Resignations. Resignations of officers or of members of the board of examiners shall be submitted in writing to the president.

Section 2. Vacancies. Vacancies in office, due to death, resignation, or other causes, other than that of the president, shall be filled by the executive board. In event the office of president becomes vacant, the vice president shall automatically move up to that office.

ARTICLE VI

Committees

Section 1. Appointment. The president shall appoint committees as provided by the bylaws or which he may deem necessary in conducting the affairs of this organization.

Section 2. Standing committees. Standing committees of this organization shall be a Steering Committee and a Committee on Certification.

ARTICLE VII

Elections

Section 1. Terms of office. The officers of this organization shall be elected for a four-year term, with the terms of those elected at the organizational meeting to expire June 30, 1968. Officers shall be elected by the executive board not later than May 31, 1968, and May 31 of subsequent four-year periods. Terms shall expire on June 30 of election years.

Section 2. Nominations. Nominations for officers may be made by any member of the organization or by the executive board and submitted to the secretary-treasurer not later than April 1 of election years.

Section 3. Members of the board of examiners. Terms of members of the board of examiners originally appointed by the president shall be for six years, with initial terms expiring June 30, 1970. Nominations for members of the board of examiners may be submitted by members residing in the respective regions to the secretary-treasurer not later than May 31 of the appointment years. The executive board shall then act on appointments but shall not be limited to such nominations. Terms shall expire on June 30 of appointment years.

ARTICLE VIII

Disbursements

The secretary-treasurer shall make such disbursements from the funds of the organization as may be authorized by the president and/or executive board.

ARTICLE IX

Official Publication

This organization may have an official publication for its reports and other material if, in the opinion of the executive board, such a publication is feasible. In the absence of an official publication, other forms of publication shall be used, as the executive board may authorize.

ARTICLE X

Amendments

Section 1. Methods of amendment. Amendments to the bylaws may be made by one of the following methods:

    (a) By a majority vote at a called meeting;

(b) by a mail vote, provided a minimum of one-half the members in good standing vote within a 30-day period and with a majority in favor.

Section 2. Proposals. Amendments to the bylaws may be proposed by one of the following methods:

(a) In the customary manner at a called meeting;

(b) in writing and signed by ten or more members in good standing for a mail vote;

(c) by the executive board.

ARTICLE XI

Parliamentary Authority

Robert's Rules of Order, current edition, shall be the parliamentary authority governing deliberations of this organization.

Committee: Jess M. Smith
Susan Christian
Frank B. Sullivan

APPENDIX C

**Present Bylaws of the
Registry of Interpreters for the Deaf, Inc.**

**(As amended January 1985, January 1986,
February 1987, August 1987, July 1989)**

ARTICLE I. PRINCIPAL OFFICE

The principal office for the transaction of the business of the corporation is fixed and located in Montgomery County, Maryland. The Board of Directors may at any time, or from time to time, change the location of the principal office from one location to another.

ARTICLE II. PURPOSES

Section 1. Principal Purposes. The principal purposes of this corporation are to initiate, sponsor, promote and execute policies and activities that will further the profession of interpretation of American Sign Language and English and the transliteration of English.

Section 2. Objectives.
A. To establish certification standards for qualified interpreters and transliterators.
B. To produce and administer certification evaluations.
C. To confer and revoke certification.
D. To maintain and promote a code of ethics for interpreters and transliterators.

E. To provide for the professional development of certified interpreters and transliterators.

F. To provide the public with information regarding interpreting and transliterating.

G. To promote, maintain and distribute a registry of certified interpreters and transliterators.

H. To prepare and distribute professional publications regarding interpreting and transliterating.

I. To raise funds to support the purposes and activities of the corporation.

J. To support the activities of organizations: of and for deaf persons, and; of and for interpreters, transliterators and translators, insofar as such activities are not in conflict with the purposes of this corporation.

K. To provide for the establishment and maintenance of affiliate chapters of the corporation.

ARTICLE III. MEMBERSHIP

Section 1. - Categories of Membership. This corporation shall have the following categories of membership:
A. Voting Members
  1. Certified Member
  2. Associate Member
B. Non-voting Members
  3. Student Member
  4. Supporting Member
  5. Organizational/Institutional Member

Section 2. - Eligibility.

A. Certified Member: any interpreter or transliterator of American Sign Language and/or English currently holding a valid certification from RID.

B. Associate Member (non-certified): Any individual who is actively engaged in the interpretation of American Sign Language and English and/or the transliteration of English, but who is not currently certified by the RID.

C. Student Member: Any non-certified individual currently enrolled in a course of study in interpretation of American Sign Language and English and the transliteration of English.

D. Supporting Member: Any non-certified individual with an interest in supporting the purposes and activities of the corporation, who does not meet eligibility requirements for Sections 2.A, 2.B, or 2.C, under Article III. Membership.

E. Organizational/Institutional Member: Any organization/institution with an interest in supporting the purposes and activities of the corporation.

Section 3. - Voting Rights.
A. Each Certified Member of this corporation shall be entitled to one vote in meetings, referenda, and elections.
B. Each Associate Member (non-certified member) of this corporation shall be entitled to one vote in meetings, referenda, and elections with the exception of referenda pertaining to evaluations, certifications, and standards/ethics.

Section 4. - Termination of Membership and/or Certification.
A. Membership: an individual's membership in the RID can be terminated for the following reasons.
    1. Suspension or Expulsion for Cause: Any certified member whose membership is suspended or revoked for cause by the Board of Directors upon recommendation of the National Certification Board and/or National Review Board of the RID will automatically be suspended or expelled from the corporation until such time as membership can be reinstated. Individuals whose membership is suspended or revoked for cause can maintain certification by payment of the certified non-member fee defined by the corporation.
    2. Non-Payment of Dues: Non-payment of dues, within thirty (30) days of due date, by a member in any category shall result in termination of membership.
B. Certification: an individual's certification in the RID can be terminated for the following reasons.
    1. Suspension or Revocation for Cause: Any certified member whose certification is suspended or revoked for cause by the Board of Directors upon recommendation of the National Certification Board and/or the National Review Board of the RID will automatically lose all rights and privileges of a certified member until such time as certification can be reinstated. Individuals whose certification is suspended or revoked for cause can maintain membership in the corporation by payment of the non-certified membership fee defined by the corporation.
    2. Non-Payment of Dues: Non-payment of dues within thirty (30) days of the due date results in invalidation of certification and a non-certified status. Individuals who fail to pay for certified membership will be treated as non-certified non-members of the corporation and thus forfeit all rights and privileges of such status.

C. Resignation: Any member may resign before the expiration of membership and/or certification by filing a written notice with the National Office of the corporation and surrendering the corporation membership and certification card. Such resignation renders both membership and certification invalid. Furthermore, such resignation shall not relieve the member of paying dues, assessments or other charges theretofore accrued, and unpaid.

D. Loss of Rights and Privileges: Upon termination of membership and/or certification, all rights and privileges immediately cease. There shall be no refund of dues or assessments. Furthermore, the corporation will publish an annual list of those individuals whose certification and/or membership has been suspended or revoked [for reasons other than non-payment of dues].

E. Appeals: Committee recommendations regarding suspension or revocation of membership and/or certification may be appealed to the National Review Board following the guidelines set forth by that Board.

Section 5. - Reinstatement.

A. Reinstatement following Suspension or Expulsion for Cause: Upon notice of reinstatement of certification and/or membership, from the National Certification Board and/or National Review Board to the National Office, a former certified member or member may apply for reinstatement.

B. Reinstatement Following Termination for Non-Payment of Dues or Resignation: Upon re-application for membership and payment of annual dues for the current year and reinstatement fees as determined by the RID Board of Directors, a member can be reinstated.

C. Application for Reinstatement: A former member who satisfies the requirements for reinstatement may make application by submitting an application form to the National Office with the appropriate fees. Upon receipt of the application form and fees, by the National Office, membership shall be reinstated and all rights and privileges shall resume.

Section 6. - Change of Membership Category. A member must change category of membership when there is a change in membership eligibility (see Article III, Section 2), upon expiration of current membership year. Furthermore, a new application must be filed along with payment of annual dues for the new category, within thirty (30) days of due date for annual dues.

Section 7. - Transfer of Membership. Membership in this corporation is not transferable or assignable. All rights of membership cease at the member's death.

Section 8. - Special Interest Groups. This corporation may establish Special Interest Groups which shall be open to all members of the corporation who meet requirements for membership as shall be defined, from time to time, by the Board of Directors and approved by the members. All Special Interest Groups must be self-sustaining. No RID corporate funds may be used to support any Special Interest Group.

Section 9. - Liabilities of Members. No individual who is now or who later becomes a member of this corporation shall be personally liable to its creditors for any indebtedness, or liability, and any and all creditors shall look only to the assets of this corporation for payment.

ARTICLE IV. MEETINGS OF MEMBERS

Section 1. - Biennial Meetings. General membership meetings shall be held biennially with a written notice of time and place of meeting to be given at least nine (9) months prior to the meeting.

Section 2. - Special Meetings. Special membership meetings may be called at any time by the Board of Directors or by written petition of not less than ten (10%) percent of the voting members of the corporation, sent to the Board of Directors. Written notice of the time and place of special meetings shall be given at least two (2) months prior to the meeting.

Section 3. - Place of Meetings. The Board of Directors may designate any one place as the place of meeting for any biennial or special meeting called.

Section 4. - Quorum.
A. Fifty-one percent (51%) of the voting membership registered to attend a biennial or any special meeting where the membership will convene to address business and,
B. Seventy-five percent (75%) of the proxy votes duly registered for the meeting.

Section 5. - Proxies. Proxies may be assigned and carried by voting members only, and must be postmarked and in written form, to the National Office sixty (60) days prior to the date of the membership meeting.

Proxies of certified members may be carried by certified members only, and proxies of associate members may be carried by other associate members or certified members only. Each voting member may represent by proxy up to one percent (1%) of the voting members in his/her membership category. Proxies in excess of one percent (1%) shall be re-assigned by the member carrying the proxies to another voting member in the same category of membership.

Section 6. - Conduct of Meetings. Unless otherwise provided for by the membership, all meetings shall be conducted according to Robert's Rules of Order (Revised).

Section 7. - Conventions. Biennial national conventions shall be held for the purposes of providing for professional development of the membership, to conduct necessary business of the corporation and to provide a forum for the exchange of information among members and the general public on or about interpretation and transliteration.

ARTICLE V. MAIL REFERENDUM

Motions may be voted on by the membership by mail referendum in the following manner:

A. Mail referenda may be drafted and submitted by the Board of Directors or by written petition of not less than ten percent (10%) of the voting members of the corporation, sent to the Board of Directors.

B. Written notice of the referendum, stating and describing all motions, procedures and deadlines for voting, shall be provided to all voting members at least sixty (60) days prior to the referendum deadline.

C. Results of mail referenda shall be determined as in Elections (Article VI, Section 8.B and 8.D).

D. Results of mail referenda shall be disseminated to the membership forty-five (45) days after the referenda deadline.

ARTICLE VI. DIRECTORS

Section 1. - Number of Directors. The number of directors shall be nine (9) unless and until the number of directors is changed by amendment to these Bylaws.

Section 2. - Composition of Board of Directors. The Board of Directors shall be comprised of President, Vice-President, Secretary/Treasurer, Member-at-Large, and five (5) Regional Representatives. In addition, the immediate past president will serve as an ex-officio member of the board for one term.

Section 3. - Limitations. Directors shall not concurrently serve as an elected officer on the Board of any affiliate chapter. Directors shall also not serve as an evaluator, monitor (assistant) or Local Evaluation Team chairperson of any RID National Evaluation System evaluation.

Section 4. - Powers. Subject to the limitations of the Articles of Incorporation, other sections of these Bylaws and of California law, all corporate powers of the corporation shall be exercised by or under the authority of, and the business and affairs of the corporation shall be controlled by, the Board of Directors. Furthermore, the specific powers shall include:

A. Unless otherwise delegated to the appointed Chief Executive Officer/Executive Director of corporation, they shall select and remove all agents and employees of the corporation, prescribe such powers and duties for them as may not be inconsistent with the law, the Articles of Incorporation, or the Bylaws; fix their compensation, and require from them security for faithful service.

B. To conduct, manage, and control the affairs and business of the corporation, and to make rules and regulations not inconsistent with law, the Articles of Incorporation, or the Bylaws.

C. To borrow money and incur indebtedness for the purposes of the corporation, and for that purpose to cause to be executed and delivered, in the corporate name, promissory notes, bonds, debentures, deeds of trust, mortgages, pledges, hypothecations, or other evidence of debts and securities.

Section 5. - Duties.
A. Directors.
    1. To perform any and all duties imposed on them collectively or individually by law, the Articles of Incorporation, by these Bylaws or by the mandate and direction of the voting membership of this corporation.
    2. To adopt, make and use a corporate seal, corporate logo; to prescribe the forms of members' certificates and membership cards, and affiliated chapters' charters.
    3. To supervise the Chief Executive Officer/Executive Director of the corporation, who will in-turn report to the Board of Directors the supervision of all subordinate officers, agents and em-

ployees of the corporation to ensure that their duties are performed properly.

4. To approve a budget, annually.

B. Officers.

   1. President.

     a. The President shall have general supervision and direction of the business affairs of the corporation. S/he shall preside at all meetings of the members and/or directors and shall have such other powers and duties as may be prescribed, from time to time, by the Board of Directors or the members.

     b. The President shall appoint such committees as may be provided for in the Bylaws and following the appointment procedures in Article IX, Section 3.; and may create such other committees as may be mandated by the membership or may be deemed necessary in promoting the purposes of the corporation.

     c. The President shall share with the Secretary/Treasurer, the Chief Executive Officer/Executive Director and designated corporate employee the right to sign checks and warrants for the withdrawal of corporate funds.

     d. The President shall represent the corporation in all activities except those expressly prohibited by law, by the Articles of Incorporation, or by the Bylaws.

     e. The president shall provide quarterly reports to the membership, including all affiliate chapters, on the actions of the Board, the financial status of the corporation, activities of committees and activities of the principal office.

     f. The President shall serve as a member of the Executive Committee.

   2. Vice-President.

     a. In the absence or disability of the president, the Vice-President shall perform all duties of the President and in so acting shall have all the powers of the President. The Vice-President shall have such other powers and perform such other duties as may be prescribed, from time to time, by the Board of Directors.

     b. The Vice President shall serve as a member of the Executive Committee.

   3. Secretary/Treasurer.

     a. The Secretary/Treasurer shall keep a full and accurate record of the proceedings of the Board of Directors, shall keep the seal of the corporation and affix it to such papers and instruments as may be required in the regular course of business, shall make service of such notices as may be necessary or proper, shall supervise the keeping of the records of the corporation, shall supervise the keeping of the records pertaining to the membership of the corporation, and shall discharge such other duties of the office as prescribed by the Board of Directors.

b. The Secretary/Treasurer shall supervise the receipt and safekeeping of all funds of the corporation and deposits that may be designated by the Board of Directors. Those funds shall be paid out only on checks of the corporation signed by the President, Secretary/Treasurer or by such officers as may be designated by the Board of Directors as authorized to sign them.

c. The Secretary/Treasurer shall serve as a member of the Executive Committee.

4. Member-at-Large.

a. The Member-At-Large shall work directly with the five Regional Representatives assisting with the coordination of activities and communication in and among regions. The Member-At-Large shall have such powers and perform such other duties as may be prescribed, from time to time, by the Board of Directors.

b. The Member-At-Large shall serve as a member of the Executive Committee.

5. Immediate Past President.

a. The immediate past President shall serve as the chairperson for the Advisory Council, as an ex-officio member of the Board of Directors and such other duties as may be prescribed, from time to time, by the Board of Directors.

C. Regional Representatives.

1. Regional Representatives shall provide reports, analyzing the President's quarterly reports of Board and committee actions and principal office activities, to their respective regions. These reports shall reflect the special issues and/or concerns of their respective regions.

2. Regional Representatives shall convene and preside at region-wide meetings.

3. Regional Representatives shall facilitate the development of region-wide activities.

4. Regional Representatives shall serve as resource persons to affiliate chapter presidents and members within their respective regions.

5. Regional Representatives shall provide quarterly reports to the Board of Directors of the activities, special issues and/or concerns of the membership within their respective regions.

Section 6. - Term of Office.
A. Directors: Officers shall be elected by ballot during biennial meeting years and their term shall commence at the conclusion of the biennial meeting, but no later than September 1 of that election year, providing they are not already serving an unfinished term of office. Regional Representatives shall be elected by ballot during nonbiennial meeting years, and their term of office shall commence thirty (30) days after elections during that year, but no later than September 1, providing they are not already serving an unfinished term of office.

B. Officers: Terms of office for President, Vice-President, Secretary/Treasurer and Member-At-Large shall be for two (2) years.

C. Regional Representatives: The term of office for Regional Representatives shall be for two (2) years, with the exception of the first term of representatives elected in accordance with Article VI, Section 6.A., which shall be for one year.

D. Consecutive Terms:

    1. Officers: No Officer shall hold the same office for more than two (2) consecutive terms.

    2. Regional Representative: No Regional Representative shall hold the same office for more than three (3) consecutive terms.

Section 7. - Qualifications.
All candidates for the Board of Directors shall have been certified members in good standing for at least four (4) years prior to candidacy. Furthermore, all candidates for Regional Representative shall have been residents of their respective regions for at least two (2) years prior to candidacy. The position of Member-at-Large shall go automatically to the immediate past President of the corporation. Should the immediate past President decline or be unavailable, the position shall go automatically to the immediate past Vice-President. Should the immediate past Vice-President decline or be unavailable for the position, it shall be opened up for nomination and election within six (6) months of vacancy. Candidates for the Member-at-Large position shall fulfill the same requirements as all candidates for Officers of the corporation.

Section 8. - Nominations.
A. Any voting member in good standing may nominate candidates for office.

B. Candidates for the offices of President, Vice-President, Secretary/Treasurer [and Member-at-Large should this position be open for nominations (see Article VI, Section 7)], must receive nominating signatures of at least twenty-five (25) voting members in good standing. These twenty-five (25) signatures shall be representative of all regions.

C. Candidates for Regional Representatives must receive nominating signatures of at least twenty-five (25) voting members in good standing. These twenty-five (25) signatures shall be from voting members within the candidates' respective regions.

D. A call for nominations, stating and describing the offices open for election and the nominations and elections procedures shall be postmarked to the membership by January first (1st) of the election year. Nominations shall be postmarked to the principal office by April first (1st) of the election year.

Section 9. - Elections.

A. Ballots shall be postmarked to the voting members by May first (1st) of the election year.

B. Ballots shall be postmarked to the principal office, or to designated office such as an accounting firm, by June first (1st) of the election year.

C. Election results and vote counts for officers shall be made public at the biennial meeting of the membership and shall be published in the first edition of the newsletter following the biennial meeting of the members. Election results and vote counts for Regional Representatives shall be published in the first edition of the newsletter following the election during non-biennial years.

D. All elections shall be determined by plurality of those eligible and voting.

Section 10. - Vacancies.

Vacancies of the Board of Directors shall exist upon the death, resignation or removal of any director, and whenever the number of directors is increased by amendment to these Bylaws.

A. Resignation: Any director may resign upon giving written notice to the President and the Secretary/Treasurer. Change of residence by a Regional Representative from one region to another, more than six months prior to completion of term of office, shall require immediate written resignation.

B. Removal of Directors:

    1. Removal Due to Legal Action: The Board of Directors may declare vacant the office of any director who has been declared of unsound mind by a final order of court, or convicted of a felony, or been found by a final order of judgment of any court to have breached any duty under Section 5230 and following of the California Nonprofit Corporation Law.

    2. Removal for Cause: A move for removal of any director may be brought by the Board of Directors or by a majority of the voting membership only after it has been established that s/he has not been acting in good faith in the fulfillment of the duties inherent in the office. A three-quarters (3/4) majority vote of the Board of Directors is required for a resolution for removal, during a meeting in which reasonable notice of action has been given to the interested party. Following resolution for removal by either the Board of Directors or the voting membership, an ad hoc review committee, mutually acceptable to the parties, shall be appointed by the Board and shall be responsible for carrying out a formal review of cause. At the review meeting, interested parties have the right to counsel.

    a. Officers: A decision for removal by the review committee and by the Board of Directors must be approved by two-thirds (2/3) of the membership, eligible and voting.

    b. Regional Representatives: A decision for removal by the review committee and by the Board of Directors must be approved by two-thirds (2/3) of that representative's region, eligible and voting.

C. Appointment to Fill a Vacancy: Any vacancy occurring in the Board of Directors and any directorship to be filled by reason of an increase in the number of directors may be filled by the affirmative vote of a majority of the remaining directors, though less than a quorum of the Board of Directors. A director appointed to fill a vacancy shall be appointed for the unexpired term of her/his predecessor in office, provided the unexpired portion of the term is not more than one (1) year. If the unexpired term is more than one (1) year a special election must be held within six (6) months of the vacancy, to fill the unexpired term. In the event of an uncontested election, the presiding officer shall cast one ballot for the nominee.

Section 11. - Regular Meetings.

A. Biennial Meetings: Biennial meetings of the Board of Directors shall be held without other notice than this bylaw, immediately before and/or after, and at the same place as, the biennial meeting of members.

B. Other Regular Meetings: Other regular meetings of the Board of Directors shall be held on a quarterly basis at such time as shall from time to time be fixed by the Board of Directors. Such meetings may be held at any place designated by the Board of Directors.

Section 12. - Special Meetings. These may be called by the President or by any two (2) Directors, with a majority vote of approval by the Board of Directors, and such meetings shall be held at the place designated by the person or persons calling the meeting, and in the absence of such designation, at the principal office of the corporation.

Section 13. - Meetings by Telephone. Any meeting, regular or special, may be held by conference telephone or similar communication equipment, so long as all directors participating in the meeting can communicate with one another, and all such directors shall be deemed to be present in person at such meetings.

Section 14. - Quorum. A majority of the Board of Directors shall constitute a quorum for the transaction of business at any meeting of the Board; but if fewer than a majority of the directors are present at said meeting, a majority of the directors present may adjourn the meeting without further notice.

Section 15. - Notice of Meetings. Annual meetings of the Board of Directors may be held without notice. Other regular meetings of the board shall be held upon a minimum of sixty (60) days' notice by first-class mail or by telephone or telegram, delivered to each director at their respective addresses as shown in the records of the corporation. Furthermore, the same notice shall be provided to the membership, in written form. Special meetings shall be held upon a minimum of seven (7) days' notice by first-class mail or by telephone or telegram, in the same manner as in the case of regular meetings. Notice of special meetings need not be given to the membership.

Section 16. - Informal Action by Directors. Any action required by law to be taken at a meeting of the directors, may be taken without a meeting if a consent in writing, setting forth the action so taken, is signed by all of the directors.

Section 17. - Majority Action as Board Action. Every act of decision done or made by a majority of the directors present at a meeting duly held at which a quorum is present is the act of the Board of Directors, unless the Articles of Incorporation or Bylaws of this corporation, or provisions of the California Nonprofit Corporation Law, particularly those provisions relating to the appointment of committees (Section 5212), approval of contracts or transaction in which a director has a material financial interest (Section 5233) and indemnification of directors (Section 5238e), require a greater percentage or different voting rules for approval of a matter by the Board.

Section 18. - Conduct of Meetings. Meetings of the Board of Directors shall be presided over by the President, or, in her/his absence, by the Vice-President, or by a Presiding Officer chosen by a majority of the directors present at the meeting. The Secretary/Treasurer shall act as recording secretary at all meetings of the board, and, in her/his absence the Presiding Officer shall appoint another person to act as secretary of the meeting.

Section 19. - Action by Unanimous Written Consent Without a Meeting. Any action required or permitted to be taken by the Board of Directors under any provision of law may be taken without a meeting, if all members of the Board individually and collectively consent in writing to such action. Such written consent or consents shall be filed with the minutes of the proceedings of the Board. Such action by written consent shall have the same force and effect as the unanimous vote of the directors. Any certificate or other document filed under any provision of law which relates to action so taken shall state that the action was taken by unanimous written consent of the Board of Directors without a meeting and that the Bylaws of this corporation authorize the Directors to so act, and such statement shall be prima facie evidence of such authority.

Section 20. - Indemnification by Corporation of Directors, Officers, Employees, and Other Agents. To the extent that a person who is, or was, a director, officer, employee, or other agent of this corporation has been successful on the merits in defense of any civil, criminal, administrative, or investigative proceeding brought to procure judgment against such person by reason of the fact that s/he is, or was an agent of the corporation, or has been successful in defense of any claim, issue or matter, therein, such person shall be indemnified against expenses actually and reasonably incurred by the person in connection with such proceeding. If such person either settles any such claim or sustains a judgment against her/him then indemnification against expenses, judgments, fines, settlements, and other amounts reasonably incurred in connection with such proceedings shall be provided by this corporation but only to the extent allowed by, and in accordance with the requirements of Section 5238 of the California Nonprofit Corporation Law.

Section 21. - Insurance for Corporate Agents. The Board of Directors may adopt a resolution authorizing the purchase and maintenance of insurance on behalf of any agent to the corporation (including a director, officer, employee, or other agent of the corporation) against any liability other than for violating provisions of law relating to self-dealing (Section 5233 of the California Nonprofit Corporation Law) asserted against or incurred by the agent in such capacity or arising out of the agent's status as such, whether or not the corporation would have the power to indemnify the agent against such liability under the provisions of Section 5238 of the California Nonprofit Corporation Law.

ARTICLE VII. REGIONAL ORGANIZATION

Section 1. - Number of Regions. The number of regions shall be five (5) unless and until the number of regions is changed by amendment to these Bylaws.

Section 2. - Composition of Regions. Regions shall be designated in such manner that they are roughly equal to each other within 100 voting members. Furthermore, designation of regions shall be assessed every five (5) years, starting in 1986 and whenever the number of regions is increased or decreased by amendment to these Bylaws. Redesignation plans must be approved by the Board of Directors.

ARTICLE VIII. AFFILIATE CHAPTERS

Section 1. - Existing Affiliate Chapter Status.
A. Any affiliate chapter located in the United States or a United States territory or protectorate at the time of adoption of these Bylaws may remain intact and autonomous as long as it so desires and so long as it complies with the provisions of these Bylaws.
B. Any member wishing to relate to the corporation through an affiliate chapter shall do so through the affiliate chapter in their state, territory, or protectorate. If there is more than one chapter in a state, territory, or protectorate, membership shall be sought in the chapter that is geographically most proximal to the member.
C. In the event that there is no affiliate chapter in their state, territory, or protectorate, any group of at least twenty (20) individuals, each of whom qualifies for membership in the corporation as a voting member, may apply for affiliation as a chapter of the corporation.
D. In the event that any group of at least twenty (20) voting members of the corporation document in writing that the affiliate chapter in their state, territory, or protectorate is unable or unwilling to meet their needs as affiliate chapter members, the group may petition the Board of Directors to grant them separate affiliate chapter status. Should the Board of Directors grant the petition, the group shall then make application for affiliation following the procedures in Article VIII, Section 2.

Section 2. - Application Procedures.
A. Each group, as defined in Article VIII, Section 1, shall submit a certified copy of its Bylaws and/or governing instruments to the National Office of the corporation. Such Bylaws and/or governing

instruments shall demonstrate that the purposes of the applicant group are substantially similar to those of the corporation, as set forth in these Bylaws.

B. Each applicant group shall submit a list of charter members and their respective qualifications for voting membership in the corporation, as set forth in Article III, Membership.

Section 3. - Application Approval.

A. Affiliate chapters of this corporation shall be created by resolution of the Board of Directors. A certificate designating an applicant group as an affiliated chapter shall be issued by the Board of Directors after the application has been approved in accordance with these Bylaws.

B. The Board of Directors shall not approve for recognition as an affiliated chapter of the corporation any applicant group which fails to state in writing its intent to be bound by the provisions of these Bylaws.

Section 4. - Offices. Elected officials, Officers and board members of any Affiliate Chapter of RID, Inc. shall be members in good standing of this Corporation. Sections numbered 4 and 5 to be changed to 5 and 6.

Section 5. - Duties and Privileges of Affiliate Chapters.

A. All affiliate chapters of this corporation shall bear a name identifying the state or region of the country in which they are located, followed by the name of this corporation (with the exception of the Texas Society of Interpreters for the Deaf - TSID was founded in 1963, one year prior to the founding of this organization), for example, the Wisconsin Chapter of the Registry of Interpreters for the Deaf.

B. All affiliated chapters of this corporation shall forward to the National Office of the corporation a copy of all amendments and modifications to the Bylaws and/or governing instruments of said chapter.

C. All affiliated chapters of this corporation shall be bound by all recommendations and resolutions of this corporation, or of the Board of Directors, so long as such recommendations and resolutions are not in conflict with the purposes of this corporation.

D. Each affiliated chapter of this corporation shall, within thirty (30) days after the expiration of each fiscal year of said chapter, forward to the National Office of the corporation a certified copy of its financial statement, including a description of the source of all receipts, and a description of all disbursements.

E. All affiliated chapters of this corporation shall comply with the laws of the States in which they are located, respectively, as well as the laws of the United States, and shall file with the appropriate governmental authorities all legal documents required to be filed.

F. Each affiliated chapter shall receive quarterly reports from the President on the actions of the Board, the financial status of the corporation, activities of committees and activities of the principal office.

G. Each affiliated chapter shall receive reports from their respective Regional Representatives analyzing the President's quarterly reports, as described in Article VI, Section 5., b., 1., e.

H. Each affiliated chapter shall be eligible to apply for Tax Exempt Status under the "umbrella" of the corporation, contingent upon pre-determined criteria, as set forth by the Internal Revenue Service.

I. Each affiliated chapter shall have the right to use the logo of the corporation as part of their respective logos.

Section 6. - Maintenance of Charter. Good standing of affiliated chapters in this corporation shall be contingent upon compliance with the duties set forth in Article VIII, Section 4 of these Bylaws, and failure to comply with same shall result in non-recognition of said affiliated chapter and revocation of its charter.

ARTICLE IX. COMMITTEES

Section 1. - Executive Committee.

A. The Executive Committee shall be comprised of the President, Vice-President, Secretary/Treasurer and Member-At-Large.

B. The Executive Committee shall be responsible for preparing the agenda prior to the full Board of Directors meeting and shall have from time to time, other duties and administrative responsibilities as prescribed by the full Board or members.

C. In the event that the full Board is unable to convene, the Executive Committee shall be given full power and authority to take action on emergency issues.

D. In addition, the Executive Committee shall conduct periodic and aperiodic appraisals of the performance of the Executive Director as requested by the Board of Directors.

Section 2. - Type and Composition of Committees. The corporation shall have Standing Committees, and may have Special and/or Ad Hoc Committees. Committees shall be composed of at least three (3) voting members, unless otherwise regulated by law, the Articles of Incorporation, or these Bylaws. No director may serve as a voting member of any committee other than the Executive Committee.

Section 3. - Appointments. Unless otherwise specified in these Bylaws, the members of all committees shall be appointed by the President upon approval of a majority Board of Directors. Furthermore, the President shall designate a member of the Board of Directors to serve as an "ex-officio" member of each committee. The President may authorize committee chairpersons to select the other members of their respective committees.

Section 4. - Standing Committees. The Board of Directors by a two-thirds (2/3) majority vote, shall have the right to establish any standing committee deemed necessary to carry out the objectives of the corporation as set forth in these Bylaws and/or mandated by the voting membership. Standing committees shall be comprised of certified members in good standing, appointed by the President upon approval of the Board of Directors. The standing committees of this corporation shall include, but not be limited to, the following:

1. Executive Committee
2. National Certification Board
3. National Testing Board
4. National Review Board
5. National Grievance Committee
6. National Bylaws Committee
7. National Convention Committee
8. Professional Development Committee
9. Professional Standards Committee
10. Public Information & Education Committee
11. Affiliate Chapter Relations Committee
12. Professional Publications Committee
13. Legislative Committee
14. Scholarship Committee

Section 5. - Special or Other Committees. The President, upon approval by the Board of Directors, shall appoint any special and/or ad hoc committees as may be deemed necessary to carry out the objectives, activities of the corporation as set forth in these Bylaws and/or as mandated by the voting membership of the corporation.

Section 6. - Term of Office. Each member of a committee shall serve until her/his successor is appointed, unless the committee shall be sooner terminated, or unless such member be removed from such committee, or unless such member cease to qualify as a member thereof, or such member resigns.

Section 7. - Vacancies. Vacancies in the membership of any committee may be filled by appointment made in like manner to Article IX, Section 3 of these Bylaws.

Section 8. - Quorum. Unless otherwise provided in these Bylaws or by resolution of the Board of Directors, a majority of the whole committee shall constitute a quorum and the action of a majority of the members present at the meeting at which a quorum is present or voting on the matter shall be the action of the committee.

Section 9. - Action of Committees. Meetings and action of committees shall be governed by, noticed, held and taken in accordance with the provision of these Bylaws that concern meetings of the Board of Directors as set forth in Article VI, Sections 11-15, with such changes in the context of such Bylaw provisions as are necessary to substitute the committee and its members for the Board of Directors and its members, except that the time for regular meetings of committees may be fixed by resolution of the Board of Directors or by the committee. The time for special meetings may also be fixed by the Board of Directors. The Board may also adopt rules and regulations pertaining to the conduct of meetings of committees to the extent that such rules and regulations are not inconsistent with the provisions of these Bylaws.

ARTICLE X. ADVISORY COUNCIL

The Board of Directors may, by a majority vote of directors then in office, designate professionals from various areas of interest and concern to the profession of interpreting, and the corporation, to serve as members of the Advisory Council, and may assign to the Advisory Council such duties as may be appropriate, so long as such duties are not in conflict with these Bylaws.

ARTICLE XI. EXECUTION OF INSTRUMENTS, DEPOSITS AND FUNDS

Section 1. - Execution of Instruments. The Board of Directors, except as otherwise provided in these Bylaws, may by resolution authorize any officer or agent of the corporation to enter into any contract or execute and deliver any instrument in the name of and on behalf of the corporation, and such authority may be general or confined to specific instances. Unless so authorized, no officer, agent, or employee shall have any power or authority to bind the corporation by any contract or engagement or to pledge its credit or to render it liable monetarily for any purpose or in any amount.

Section 2. - Promissory Notes. In order to authorize the signing of any promissory note, the Board of Directors must cast a two-thirds (2/3) majority vote for approval of such authorization.

Section 3. - Checks and Notes. Except as otherwise specifically determined by resolution of the Board of Directors, or as otherwise required by law, checks, drafts, orders for payment of money, and other evidence of indebtedness of the corporation, shall be signed by the Secretary/Treasurer and countersigned by the President.

Section 4. - Deposits. All funds of the corporation shall be deposited from time to time to the credit of the corporation in such banks, trust companies, or other depositories as the Board of Directors may designate.

Section 5. - Gifts. The Board of Directors may accept on behalf of the corporation any contribution, gift, bequest or device for the nonprofit or public purpose of the corporation.

ARTICLE XII. CORPORATE RECORDS, REPORTS AND SEALS

Section 1. - Maintenance of Corporate Records.
A. Minutes of all meetings of Directors, committees of the corporation and meetings of members, indicating the time and place of such meetings, whether regular or special, how called, the notice given, and the names of those present and the proceedings thereof.
B. Adequate and correct books and records of accounts, including accounts of its properties and business transactions and accounts of its assets, liabilities, receipts, disbursements, gains, and losses.
C. A record of its members, indicating their names and addresses, the category of membership held by each member, qualifying criteria for membership, the termination date of any membership and certification and related information.
D. A copy of the corporation's Articles of Incorporation and Bylaws as amended to date, which shall be open to inspection by the members

of the corporation at all reasonable times during business hours.

Section 2. - Corporate Seal. The Board of Directors may adopt, use, and at will alter, a corporate seal. Such seal shall be kept at the principal office of the corporation. Failure to affix the seal to corporate instruments, however, shall not affect the validity of any such instrument, unless such affixing of the corporate seal shall be required by law.

Section 3. - Corporate Logo. The Board of Directors may adopt, use, and at will alter, a corporate logo. Such logo shall be duly registered and used by the corporation and its affiliated chapters for official and/or approved purposes only. The corporate logo may not be used by an individual member for their personal use.

Section 4. - Directors' Inspection Rights. Every director shall have the absolute right at any reasonable time to inspect and copy all books, records and documents of every kind and to inspect the physical properties of the corporation.

Section 5. - Members' Inspection Rights. Each and every member shall have the following inspection rights, for a purpose reasonably related to such person's interest as a member:

A. To inspect and copy the record of all members' names, addresses and voting rights, at reasonable times, upon submitting a written request to the National Office, with a ten (10) business days' notice, which request shall state the purpose for which the inspection is requested.

B. To obtain from the corporation, upon written request and payment of a reasonable charge, as determined by the National Office, a list of the names, addresses and voting rights of those members entitled to vote in elections as of the most recent record date for which the list has been compiled or as of the date specified by the member subsequent to the date, if denied. The request shall state the purpose for which the list is requested. The membership list shall be made available on or before the latter of ten (10) business days after the request is received or after the date specified therein as of which the list is to be compiled.

C. Inspect at any reasonable time the books, records, or minutes of proceedings of the members or of the Board or committees of the Board, upon written request to the corporation by the member, and with a ten (10) business days' notice, for a purpose reasonably related to such person's interests as a member.

Section 6. - Right to Copy and Make Extracts. Any inspection under the provisions of this Article may be made in person or by agent or attorney and the right to inspection includes the right to copy and make extracts.

Section 7. - Annual Report. The Board of Directors shall cause an Annual Report to be furnished by the designated officers not later than ninety (90) days after the close of the corporation's fiscal year to all corporation's directors and members. Such report shall contain the following information in appropriate detail:

A. The assets and liabilities, including the trust funds, of the corporation as of the close of the fiscal year.

B. The principal changes in assets and liabilities, including trust funds, during the fiscal year.

C. The revenue or receipts of the corporation, both unrestricted and restricted to particular purposes, for the fiscal year.

D. The expenses or disbursements of the corporation, both for general and restricted purposes, during the fiscal year. The annual report shall be accompanied by any report thereon by independent accountants, or, if there is no such report, the certificate of an authorized officer of the corporation that such statements were prepared without audit from the books and records of the corporation.

ARTICLE XIII. FISCAL YEAR OF THE CORPORATION

The fiscal year of the corporation shall begin on the first (1st) day of July and end on the thirtieth (30th) day of June in each year.

ARTICLE XIV. FEES, DUES AND ASSESSMENTS

Each member in good standing must pay, within the time and on the conditions set by the Board of Directors and these Bylaws, the annual dues in amounts to be fixed from time to time by the Board of Directors. The Board of Directors shall not increase or decrease membership dues by more than ten percent (10%) without a majority vote of the membership either at the biennial meeting or by mail referendum. The dues shall be equal for all members of each category, but different dues may be set for each category.

Section 1. - Payment of Dues. Payment of dues shall be in advance of the first (1st) day of July of each fiscal year.

Section 2. - Reinstatement Fees, Dues in Arrears and Late Fees. The Board of Directors may determine from time to time the amount of a reinstatement fee, if any, and the manner in which such fees must be paid. Furthermore, the Board of Directors may determine and assign the payment of a reasonable late fee. Dues are in arrears as of August first (1st) of each fiscal year. Reinstatement following termination shall be contingent upon payment of dues in arrears and such reinstatement and/or late fees as shall be assigned by the Board of Directors.

ARTICLE XV. AMENDMENT OF BYLAWS

Section 1. - Amendment of Members. New Bylaws or amendments to these Bylaws must be reviewed by the National Bylaws Committee. New Bylaws may be adopted or these Bylaws may be amended or repealed by approval of two-thirds (2/3) majority of the voting members of the corporation, eligible and voting during a regular or special meeting of the membership or through the mail referendum. However, any amendment which would materially and adversely affect the rights of any other category of members as to voting or transfer, differently than such action affects another category, must be approved by a two-thirds (2/3) majority of the members of such affected category. Furthermore, no amendment may be voted on during the same meeting, whether regular or special, at which such amendment is proposed, without prior notice.

Section 2. - Transitory Provisions. In any transition period, the Board of Directors shall, by a majority vote of the Directors, prescribe the necessary mechanisms for implementing any changes resulting from changes in the Bylaws.

ARTICLE XVI. VETO POWERS OF THE MEMBERS

Any decision of the Board of Directors may be vetoed by a two thirds (2/3) majority vote of those eligible and voting during a regular or special meeting of the membership (See Article IV) or through mail referendum (See Article V).

ARTICLE XVII. AMENDMENT OF THE ARTICLES OF INCORPORATION

Amendments to the Articles of Incorporation may be adopted by a recommendation of the Board of Directors and the approval of two-thirds (2/3) of the voting members eligible and voting during a regular or special meeting of the membership or through mail referendum.

ARTICLE XVIII. DISSOLUTION OF THE CORPORATION

Upon the dissolution or winding up of this corporation, its assets remaining after payment of, or provisions for payment of, all debts and liabilities of this corporation shall be distributed to a non-profit fund, foundation, or corporation that is organized and operated exclusively for educational purposes which has established its tax-exempt status under Section 501 (c) (3) of the Internal Revenue Code, as amended.

APPENDIX D

ORIGINAL CODE OF ETHICS

1. The interpreter shall be a person of high moral character, honest, conscientious, trustworthy, and of emotional maturity. He shall guard confidential information and not betray confidences which have been entrusted to him.

2. The interpreter shall maintain an impartial attitude during the course of his interpreting avoiding interjecting his own views unless he is asked to do so by a party involved.

3. The interpreter shall interpret, faithfully and to the best of his ability, always conveying the thought, intent, and spirit of the speaker. He shall remember the limits of his particular function and not go beyond his responsibility.

4. The interpreter shall recognize his own level of proficiency and use discretion in accepting assignments, seeking for the assistance of other interpreters when necessary.

5. The interpreter shall adopt a conservative manner of dress upholding the dignity of the profession and not drawing undue attention to himself.

6. The interpreter shall use discretion in the matter of accepting compensation for services and be willing to provide services in situations where funds are not available. Arrangements should be made on a professional basis for adequate remuneration in court cases comparable to that provided for interpreters of foreign languages.

7. The interpreter shall never encourage deaf persons to seek legal or other decisions in their favor merely because the interpreter is sympathetic to the handicap of deafness.

8. In the case of legal interpreting, the interpreter shall inform the court when the level of literacy of the deaf person involved is such that literal interpretation is not possible and the interpreter is having to grossly paraphrase and restate both what is said to the deaf person and what he is saying to the court.

9. The interpreter shall attempt to recognize the various types of assistance needed by the deaf and to do his best to meet the particular need. Those who do not understand the language of signs may require assistance through written communication. Those who understand manual communication may be assisted by means of translating (rendering the original presentation verbatim), or interpreting (paraphrasing, defining, and explaining, or making known the will of the speaker without regard to the original language used).

10. Recognizing his need for professional improvement, the interpreter will join with professional colleagues for the purpose of sharing new knowledge and developments, to seek to understand the implications of deafness and the deaf person's particular needs, broaden his education and knowledge of life, and develop both his expressive and his receptive skills in interpreting and translating.

11. The interpreter shall seek to uphold the dignity and purity of the language of signs. He shall also maintain a readiness to learn and to accept new signs, if these are necessary to understanding.

12. The interpreter shall take the responsibility of educating the public regarding the deaf whenever possible recognizing that many misunderstandings arise because of the general lack of public knowledge in the area of deafness and communication of the deaf.

PRESENT CODE OF ETHICS

The Registry of Interpreters for the Deaf, refers to individuals who may perform one or more of the following services:

Interpret

Spoken English to American Sign Language
American Sign Language to Spoken English

Transliterate

Spoken English to Manually Coded English/Pidgin Sign English
Manually Coded English/Pidgin Sign English to Spoken English
Spoken English to Paraphrased Non-audible Spoken English

Gesticulate/Mime, etc.

Spoken English to Gesture, Mime, etc.
Gesture, Mime, etc. to Spoken English

The Registry of Interpreters for the Deaf, Inc. has set forth the following principles of ethical behavior to protect and guide the interpreter/transliterator, the consumers (hearing and hearing impaired) and the profession, as well as to insure for all the right to communicate.

This Code of Ethics applies to all members of the Registry of Interpreters for the Deaf, Inc. and all certified non-members.

While these are general guidelines to govern the performance of the interpreter/transliterator generally, it is recognized that there are ever increasing numbers of highly specialized situations that demand specific explanation It is envisioned that the R.I.D., Inc. will issue appropriate guidelines.

Code of Ethics

INTERPRETER/TRANSLITERATOR SHALL KEEP ALL ASSIGNMENT-RELATED INFORMATION STRICTLY CONFIDENTIAL.

Guidelines:

Interpreter/transliterators shall not reveal information about any assignment, including the fact that the service is being performed.

Even seemingly unimportant information could be damaging in the wrong hands. Therefore, to avoid this possibility, interpreter/transliterators must not say anything about any assignment. In cases where meetings or information becomes a matter of public record, the interpreter/transliterator shall use discretion in discussing such meetings or information.

If a problem arises between the interpreter/transliterator and either person involved in an assignment, the interpreter/transliterator should first discuss it with the person involved. If no solution can be reached, then both should agree on a third person who could advise them.

When training new trainees by the method of sharing actual experiences, the trainers shall not reveal any of the following information:

— name, sex, age, etc. of the consumer

— day of the week, time of the day, time of the year the situation took place

— location, including city, state or agency

— other people involved

— unnecessary specifics about the situation

It only takes a minimum amount of information to identify the parties involved.

INTERPRETER/TRANSLITERATORS SHALL RENDER THE MESSAGE FAITHFULLY, ALWAYS CONVEYING THE CONTENT AND SPIRIT OF THE SPEAKER, USING LANGUAGE MOST READILY UNDERSTOOD BY THE PERSON(S) WHOM THEY SERVE.

Guidelines:

Interpreter/transliterators are not editors and must transmit everything that is said in exactly the same way it was intended. This is especially difficult when the interpreter disagrees with what is being said, or feels uncomfortable when profanity is being used. Interpreter/transliterators must remember that they are not responsible for what is said, only for conveying it accurately. If the interpreter/transliterator's own feelings interfere with rendering the message accurately, he/she shall withdraw from the situation.

While working from Spoken English to Sign or Non-audible Spoken English, the interpreter/transliterator should communicate in the manner most easily understood or preferred by the deaf and hard of hearing person(s), be it American Sign Language, Manually Coded English, fingerspelling, paraphrasing in Non-audible Spoken English, gesturing, drawing, or writing, etc. It is important for the interpreter/transliterator and deaf or hard of hearing person(s) to spend some time adjusting to each other's way of communicating prior to the actual assignment. When working from Sign or Non-audible Spoken English, the interpreter/transliterator shall speak the language used by the hearing person in spoken form, be it English, Spanish, French, etc.

INTERPRETER/TRANSLITERATORS SHALL NOT COUNSEL, ADVISE, OR INTERJECT PERSONAL OPINIONS.

Guidelines:

Just as interpreter/transliterators may not omit anything which is said, they may not add anything to the situation, even when they are asked to do so by other parties involved.

An interpreter/transliterator is only present in a given situation because two or more people have difficulty communicating, and thus the interpreter/transliterator's only function is to facilitate communication. He/she shall not become personally involved because in so doing he/she accepts some responsibility for the outcome, which does not rightly belong to the interpreter/transliterator.

How about clarification

INTERPRETER/TRANSLITERATORS SHALL ACCEPT ASSIGNMENTS USING DISCRETION WITH REGARD TO SKILL, SETTING, AND THE CONSUMERS INVOLVED.

Guidelines:

Interpreter/transliterators shall only accept assignments for which they are qualified. However, when an interpreter/transliterator shortage exists and the only available interpreter/transliterator does not possess the necessary skill for a particular assignment, this situation should be explained to the consumer. If the consumers agree that services are needed regardless of skill level, then the available interpreter/transliterator will have to use his/her best judgement about accepting or rejecting the assignment.

Certain situations may prove uncomfortable for some interpreter/transliterators and clients. Religious, political, racial or sexual differences, etc., can adversely affect the facilitating task. Therefore, an interpreter/transliterator shall not accept assignments which he/she knows will involve such situations.

Interpreter/transliterators shall generally refrain from providing services in situations where family members, or close personal or professional relationships may affect impartiality, since it is difficult to mask inner feelings. Under these circumstances, especially in legal settings, the ability to prove oneself unbiased when challenged is lessened. In emergency situations, it is realized that the interpreter/transliterator may have to provide services for family members, friends, or close business associates. However, all parties should be informed that the interpreter/transliterator may not become personally involved in the proceedings.

INTERPRETER/TRANSLITERATORS SHALL REQUEST COMPENSATION FOR SERVICES IN A PROFESSIONAL AND JUDICIOUS MANNER.

Guidelines:

Interpreter/transliterators shall be knowledgeable about fees which are appropriate to the profession, and be informed about the current suggested fee schedule of the national organization. A sliding scale of hourly and daily rates has been established for interpreter/transliterators in many areas. To determine the appropriate fee, interpreter/transliterators should know their own level of skill, level of certification, length of experience, nature of the assignment and the local cost of living index.

There are circumstances when it is appropriate for interpreter/transliterators to provide services without charge. This should be done with discretion, taking care to preserve the self-respect of the consumers. Consumers should not feel that they are recipients of charity. When providing gratis services, care should be taken so that the livelihood of other interpreter/transliterators will be protected. A free-lance interpreter/transliterator may depend on this work for a living and therefore must charge for services rendered, while persons with other full-time work may perform the service as a favor without feeling a loss of income.

INTERPRETER/TRANSLITERATORS SHALL FUNCTION IN A MANNER APPROPRIATE TO THE SITUATION.

Guidelines:

Interpreter/transliterators shall conduct themselves in such a manner that brings respect to themselves, the consumers and the national organization. The term "appropriate manner" refers to:

(a) dressing in a manner that is appropriate for skin tone and is not distracting

(b) conducting oneself in all phases of an assignment in a manner befitting a professional.

INTERPRETER/TRANSLITERATORS SHALL STRIVE TO FURTHER KNOWLEDGE AND SKILLS THROUGH PARTICIPATION IN WORKSHOPS, PROFESSIONAL MEETINGS, INTERACTION WITH PROFESSIONAL COLLEAGUES AND READING OF CURRENT LITERATURE IN THE FIELD.

INTERPRETER/TRANSLITERATORS, BY VIRTUE OF MEMBERSHIP IN OR CERTIFICATION BY THE R.I.D., INC. SHALL STRIVE TO MAINTAIN HIGH PROFESSIONAL STANDARDS IN COMPLIANCE WITH THE CODE OF ETHICS.

APPENDIX E

RID Officers and Board Members, 1964-1989

1964 - 1968

President	Kenneth F. Huff
Vice President	Elizabeth Benson
Secretary/Treasurer	Virginia Lewis
Members at Large	Frank Sullivan
	Lillian Beard

1968 - 1972

President	Ralph F. Neesam
Vice President	Mrs. Mildred Johnson
Secretary/Treasurer	Mrs. Fannie Lang
Members at Large	Dr. Elizabeth Benson
	Thomas Dillon
	Kenneth F. Huff

1972 - 1974

President	Carl J. Kirchner
Vice President	Celia Warshawsky
Secretary	John Shipman
Treasurer	Lucile Olson
Board Members	Edna Adler
	Ralph Neesam
	James Stangarone

144

1974 - 1976

President	Carl J. Kirchner
Vice President	Celia Warshawsky
Secretary	John Shipman
Treasurer	Lucile Olson
Board Members	Ralph Neesam
	James Stangarone
	William Peace

1976 - 1978

President	Carl J. Kirchner (Resigned in 1978)
Vice President	James Stangarone
Secretary	Betty Edwards
Treasurer	Roy Holcomb
Board Members	Agnes Foret
	Willard Madsen
	Evelyn Zola

1978 - 1980

President	James Stangarone
Vice President	Harry Murphy
Secretary	Agnes T. Foret
Treasurer	William Peace
Board Members	Judie D. Husted
	Dennis Cokely
	Evelyn Zola

1980 - 1982

President	Judie D. Husted
Vice President	Edward E. Corbett, Jr.
Secretary	Becky Carlson
Treasurer	Ruth Sandefur
Board Members	Agnes T. Foret
	Anna Maria Rinaldi
	Rita DeVries
	Donald G. Renzulli
	(replaced Rita DeVries)

*1982 - 1983

President	Judie D. Husted
Vice President	Edward E. Corbett, Jr.
Secretary	Becky Carlson
Treasurer	Donald G. Renzulli
Board	Agnes T. Foret
	Janice Hawkins
	Bob Alcorn

1983 - 1985

President		Dennis Cokely
Vice President		Anna Witter-Merrithew
Secretary-Treasurer		Barbara B. Brasel
Regional Representatives	I	Barbara B. Brasel
	II	Eileen Simpson (Resigned, replaced by Jerry Conner)
	III	Susan Arneson
	IV	Janice Hawkins
	V	Donald G. Renzulli

1985 - 1987

President		Dennis Cokely
Vice President		Anna Witter-Merrithew
Secretary-Treasurer		Donald G. Renzulli (Resigned, replaced by Shirley Herald)
Regional Representatives	I	Gary Mowl
	II	Bill Woodrick
	III	Ken Rust
	IV	Robin Byers
	V	Randy Jordan
	At Large:	Margaret Ransom

---

* It was decided at the Hartford Convention, 1982, to hold biennial conventions in odd-numbered years beginning with the Denver Convention, 1983.

1987 - 1989

President		Anna Witter-Merrithew
Vice President		Margaret Ransom
Secretary-Treasurer		Steven Fritsch-Rudser
Regional Representatives	I	Gary Mowl
	II	Marie Griffin
	III	Gail Bedessem
	IV	Daniel Pokorny
	V	Randy Jordan
At Large:		Ken Rust

1989 - 1991

President		Jan Kanda
Vice President		Gail Bedessem
Secretary-Treasurer		Daniel Pokorny (Deceased)/Janet Bailey
Regional Representatives	I	Kellie Mills/Christopher Felo
	II	Marie Griffin/Brenda Dencer
	III	Gail Partridge
	IV	Daniel D. Burch
	V	Gary Sanderson/Sharon Vickers
At Large:		Aaron Gorelick

RID Executive Directors

1967 - 1970	Albert T. Pimentel
1971 - 1972	Emil S. Ladner
1973 - 1981	Richard Dirst served as Public Relations Director/Interpreter
1981 - 1982	Richard Dirst
1982 - 1985	W.F. Roy III
1985 - 1989	Donald D. Roose
1989 - Present	Sylvia A. Straub

Distinguished Service Award Recipients

1970 - Elizabeth Benson and Kenneth Huff
1972 - Ralph Neesam and Lou Fant
1974 - Betty Edwards
1976 - Lucille Olson
1978 - Carl Kirchner
1980 - Agnes Foret and James Stangarone
1982 - Lillian Beard
1983 - Barbara E. Brasel
1985 - (Not awarded)
1987 - (Not awarded)
1989 - Viginia Hughes and Paul Culton

Honorary Members

1972 - Edgar Lowell
1974 - Ralph Hoag, Nanette Fabray
1976 - Uriel Jones, Henry Olson, William Stokoe
1978 - Fannie Lang, Edna Kahl
1980 - William Castle
1982 - (Not awarded)
1983 - Etilvia Arjona
1985 - Harlan Lane
1987 - (Not awarded)
1989 - (Not awarded)

APPENDIX F

RID Conventions

1970 - Delavan, Wisconsin
1972 - Long Beach, California
1974 - Seattle, Washington
1976 - St. Petersburg, Florida
1978 - Rochester, New York
1980 - Cincinnati, Ohio
1982 - Hartford, Connecticut
1983 - Denver, Colorado
1985 - San Diego, California
1987 - St. Paul, Minnesota
1989 - El Paso, Texas

APPENDIX G

RID Periodicals

Periodicals for RID members have had varying titles at different times. Listed here are the titles and years during which they were published by those titles.

Newsletter   October, 1966 - January, 1967; two issues

The RIDer   April, 1967 - November, 1967; three issues in April, June, and August

RID Newsletter   November, 1967 - Spring Issue, 1970

Interprenews   Spring Issue, 1970 - August, 1979; from 1972 until 1976, the *Interprenews* appeared as a special section in *The Deaf American,* the NAD periodical

VIEWS   August, 1979 - Present